The Shak

THE SHAKESPEARE HANDBOOKS

Series Editor: John Russell Brown

PUBLISHED

John Russell Brown	*Macbeth*
Paul Edmondson	*Twelfth Night*
Christopher McCullough	*The Merchant of Venice*
Lesley Wade Soule	*As You Like It*

FORTHCOMING

Roger Apfelbaum	*Much Ado About Nothing*
John Russell Brown	*Hamlet*
David Carnegie	*Julius Caesar*
Bridget Escolme	*Antony and Cleopatra*
Kevin Ewert	*Henry V*
Trevor Griffiths	*The Tempest*
Stuart Hampton-Reeves	*Measure for Measure*
Margaret Jane Kidnie	*The Taming of the Shrew*
Paul Prescott	*Richard III*
Edward L. Rocklin	*Romeo and Juliet*
Martin White	*A Midsummer Night's Dream*

The Shakespeare Handbooks

Twelfth Night

Paul Edmondson

First published 2005 by
PALGRAVE MACMILLAN
Houndmills, Basingstoke, Hampshire RG21 6XS and
175 Fifth Avenue, New York, N.Y. 10010
Companies and representatives throughout the world

PALGRAVE MACMILLAN is the global academic imprint of the Palgrave Macmillan division of St. Martin's Press, LLC and of Palgrave Macmillan Ltd. Macmillan® is a registered trademark in the United States, United Kingdom and other countries. Palgrave is a registered trademark in the European Union and other countries.

ISBN-13: 978–1–4039–3386–7 hardback
ISBN 10: 1–4039–3386–3   hardback
ISBN-13: 978–1–4039–2094–2 paperback
ISBN 10: 1–4039–2094–X   paperback

This book is printed on paper suitable for recycling and made from fully managed and sustained forest sources.

A catalogue record for this book is available from the British Library.

A catalog record for this book is available from the Library Congress.

10   9   8   7   6   5   4   3   2   1
14   13   12   11   10   09   08   07   06   05

Printed and bound in China

Contents

General Editor's Preface

The Shakespeare Handbooks provide an innovative way of studying the theatrical life of the plays. The commentaries, which are their core feature, enable a reader to envisage the words of a text unfurling in performance, involving actions and meanings not readily perceived except in rehearsal or performance. The aim is to present the plays in the environment for which they were written and to offer an experience as close as possible to an audience's progressive experience of a production.

While each book has the same range of contents, their authors have been encouraged to shape them according to their own critical and scholarly understanding and their first-hand experience of theatre practice. The various chapters are designed to complement the commentaries: the cultural context of each play is presented together with quotations from original sources; the authority of its text or texts is considered with what is known of the earliest performances; key performances and productions of its subsequent stage history are both described and compared. The aim in all this has been to help readers to develop their own informed and imaginative view of a play in ways that supplement the provision of standard editions and are more user-friendly than detailed stage histories or collections of criticism from diverse sources.

Further volumes are in preparation so that, within a few years, the Shakespeare Handbooks will be available for all the plays that are frequently studied and performed.

John Russell Brown
January 2005

Preface

Twelfth Night is for me a quintessentially Shakespearian play, with its
lyricism of both verse and prose, its many-moodedness, its mixture
of laughter and sadness, its theatrical power and sublime inconse-
quentiality. It is also vibrantly funny, as much for its word play as for
its comic situations.

As a child, I remember finding particular resonance in the play's
title and the festival it evokes. It captured my imagination and
seemed to promise a magical story about Christmas; it conveyed,
too, echoes of a clock striking midnight. The sense of longing and
yearning, which many years later I have come to love about critical
approaches to *Twelfth Night*, on both page and stage, started long
before I ever saw or read it. In 1995, just after my finals at the
University of Durham, I played Fabian in an outdoor production
which toured around stately homes and gardens in Wales,
Lancashire, and the Lake District. I can still see and hear the voices
and movement of that cast each time I dip into the play and imagine
its performance.

I should like to record my gratitude to: Dr Susan Brock; Karin
Brown; Dr Paula Byrne, for the 'babbling gossip' of friendship;
Michael Dembowicz, RSC Company Manager, who made it possible
for me to consult the prompt-book of the 2005 production between
rehearsals; my parents Kathleen and Rowland Edmondson, whose
marriage 'golden time convents'; Robert Ewart; Helen Hargest; Sarah
Hosking; Roger Howells, for sharing his insights and experience
from the years he was Production Manager with the Royal
Shakespeare Company; Professor Christa Jansohn; Jane Lapotaire;
Dr Tom Matheson and Angela Cutrale for their fresh translation of
Gl'Ingannati; Sylvia Morris; Marian Pringle; Roger Pringle, the

Director of the Shakespeare Birthplace Trust, for his kind understanding and encouragement of the project; Dr Paul Prescott,
Amanda Jenkins and Dr Nick Walton, whose ever-encouraging
friendship has supported me along the way with present mirth and
present laughter; Professor Carol Rutter; James Shaw; Erin Sullivan;
Greg and Mary Wells for taking me to Lyme Regis out of season, and
Amy Miller, who read the play out loud with me as the waves broke
on the shore; Professor Stanley Wells, who was always available to
listen, discuss my work, and offer wise advice; and the librarians of
the Shakespeare Centre and the Shakespeare Institute, Stratford-
upon-Avon, for many courtesies. Finally, I am grateful to Professor
John Russell Brown, as General Editor of the series, for his patience,
encouragement, and trust, and for his many invaluable suggestions.

The standard critical edition used for all points of reference to
Twelfth Night, unless otherwise stated, is that edited by Roger Warren
and Stanley Wells for the multi-volume Oxford Shakespeare series
(1994); references to other Shakespearian works are to *The Oxford
Shakespeare: The Complete Works* (1986; 2nd edition 2005). These
editions are listed in the Bibliography. The text of *Twelfth Night* in the
Norton Shakespeare is identical to that in the Oxford edition.

P.M.E.

1 *The Text and Early Performances*

It is the Feast of Candlemas (2 February) 1602: the official end of Christmas, as far as the church calendar is concerned. The Lord Chamberlain's Men have an important engagement this evening. As part of a seasonal celebration they have been asked by the authorities of the Middle Temple (a law school on the Strand in London) to present one of their latest plays. Shakespeare probably wrote *Twelfth Night or What You Will* during 1601. John Manningham, one of the students, then in his fourth year of training, aged twenty-seven, provides the earliest record of a performance of the play in his notebook (often referred to by scholars as his diary). Although almost certainly not the play's premiere, it was no doubt an evening of high spirits:

> At our feast we had a play called ~~mid~~ *Twelfth Night, or What You Will*, much like *The Comedy of Errors* or *Menaechmi* in Plautus, but most like and near to that in Italian called *Inganni*. A good practice in it to make the steward believe his lady widow was in love with him, by counterfeiting a letter as from his lady, in general terms telling him what she liked best in him, and prescribing his gesture in smiling, his apparel, etc., and then when he came to practise, making believe they took him to be mad. (based on *Twelfth Night*, Arden 2nd series, p. xxvi, see also Manningham, *Diary*, p. 48)

Manningham seems familiar with the company's other work. *The Comedy of Errors* was performed at another Inn of Court, Gray's Inn, on 28 December 1594; Manningham might have been present on that occasion, too. The correction in the manuscript '~~mid~~' suggests that he might have been going to mention *Midsummer Night's Dream*, or even *Midnight*: an association inspired by the play's title, or even the time at which the evening finished. Manningham is accurate about *What*

You Will as the alternative title, which suggests that Shakespeare himself wanted his work to become known by both from an early stage. *What You Will* might have served to relate it to, but distinguish it from, two earlier works: *Much Ado About Nothing* and *As You Like It*.

Manningham's reference to Plautus's Roman comedy shows his experience of the Elizabethan grammar school education. Scholars have debated the implications of his mentioning the Italian '*Inganni*'. This could refer to *Gl'Inganni* ('The Mistakes') by Nicolò Secchi (first published in Florence in 1562). More likely, Manningham is using a generic title for an Italian play about mistaken identity and is actually calling to mind *Gl'Ingannati*, which is more readily identifiable as a source for *Twelfth Night* (see Chapter 2). His inaccurate description of a widow (presumably Olivia) no doubt relates to the actor's black costume. Either Manningham was not paying sufficient attention to the words (or, because of the nature of the occasion, and surrounded by boisterous fellow students, he *could* not), or Shakespeare later clarified this point and revised the text. The 'counterfeiting a letter as from his lady, in general terms', and how this leads to the victimization of a servant, obviously appealed to Manningham's evolving legal sensibilities and insights.

Shakespeare himself was probably among the cast, which would have included at least fourteen actors, three of whom were boys playing the female roles (Olivia, Viola and Maria). It is possible that Sebastian was also played by a boy (rather than a man) in order to emphasize the similarity between the twins. Robert Armin, the company's new comic actor (and already by this time quite famous in his own right), might have played the part of Feste. The company's other famous comedian, Will Kemp, had sold his share in the Globe theatre in 1599 and Feste requires a different kind of fooling from that of Shakespeare's (Kemp's) previous clowns. The actor playing Feste also needs to be able to sing. J. M. Lothian and T. W. Craik (the 1975 Arden editors) notice that Sir Toby and Sir Andrew are a similar pairing to Dogberry and Verges in *Much Ado About Nothing*, who were played by Will Kemp and Richard Cowley. Some scholars believe that the distinctly thin actor John Sincler played Sir Andrew Aguecheek (on the evidence that there are other thin characters in Shakespeare plays of this period: Dr Pinch in *The Comedy of Errors*,

Cassius in *Julius Caesar*, Slender in *The Merry Wives of Windsor*), but this cannot be proved. With a minimum cast of fourteen, though, Shakespeare seems to have been interested in a well-populated stage: a comedy of diverse individuals. There are at least thirteen people on stage in the final scene: all the characters except Maria (whose absence is difficult to explain, since the role cannot easily double with any of the others). Experimental productions could double Maria with either Orsino or Sebastian, but not without some gimmick or rearrangement of the text (she appears too soon after the exit of both men). Only the very minor roles in *Twelfth Night* can reasonably double (for example, the Sea Captain with the Priest, the Officers with Curio and Valentine). It is a company play, an evenly spread, finely balanced drama.

The Middle Temple that Shakespeare knew was largely destroyed in the Second World War, but faithfully restored. In 2002, Shakespeare's Globe performed an all-male *Twelfth Night* there (anachronistically without any boy actors), four hundred years after Manningham had seen it. In chapter 9 of his reconstruction of early modern performances, *Enter the Whole Army: A Pictorial Study of Shakespearean Staging, 1576–1616*, C. Walter Hodges suggests that after the students' supper, the tables and their candles were cleared away, and the chandelier was lit and raised high to maximize the lighting. At one end of the Middle Temple's long hall is an ornately carved draught screen with three doors (entrances) in it and a gallery above (for the musicians), resembling something of the back of the stage in an Elizabethan playhouse. Hodges plausibly imagines a box hedge being brought onto the stage across the central door for Sir Toby, Sir Andrew and Fabian to hide behind, and a bench being placed in front of it for Malvolio to sit on and read the letter. One of the entrances might have been curtained to represent Malvolio's dark confinement in Act IV, scene ii. In the Globe theatre, the three of them might have concealed themselves in the upper balcony area, or hidden behind the two pillars for the eavesdropping scene. It is equally likely that they hid in front of them, placing Malvolio centre stage, and ensuring that their reactions were facing a greater proportion of the audience. The trap-door could have been used for Malvolio's prison. The two side doors onto the stage could have been used for great effect with the sudden and successive appearances of the twins, a similar staging effect being desirable for *The Comedy of Errors*.

Only a small number of props are required to stage *Twelfth Night*: all the essential ones are included in Table 1. The precise line(s) at which each of the props are used will be determined by a production, rather than by an edition, so readers should begin to imagine these moments for themselves when thinking about the play in performance.

Leslie Hotson propounded a theory in *The First Night of 'Twelfth Night'* (1954) that the date of the first performance came a year earlier on 6 January 1601. His wide-ranging historical and biographical survey is inspired by two facts. First, that the Lord Chamberlain's Men were paid for presenting a play at Whitehall on that day. Secondly, that this entertainment coincided with a visit to Elizabeth's court from Virginio Orsino, Duke of Bracciano. Hotson came across a full narrative description of the entertainments presented to this Italian Orsino in the papers of the Duke of Northumberland, though it was not quite full enough to reveal what play was performed for the occasion. His study is at best historically engaging and at worst cryptic. Hotson's theory is that Shakespeare was commissioned to write a play during his appearance at court on St Stephen's night (26 December) 1600 and that since he completed it in eleven days he called it *Twelfth Night*, a satirical drama which playfully mocks William Knollys, Earl of Banbury (as Malvolio), as well as Virginio Orsino, Duke of Bracciano (as Orsino), and Elizabeth herself (as Olivia). We shall never know. Hotson's theory seems as 'high fantastical' (I.i.15) as the play itself, but it is possible that Shakespeare named Orsino after the Italian duke.

There are far more solid contingencies which may reveal something of *Twelfth Night*'s early performance history. Feste's songs may not be by Shakespeare; Robert Armin might have imported them into the play. It is possible that the earliest audiences already knew a version of 'O Mistress Mine', and of 'Hey Robin'. 'Farewell dear heart' seems to be closely based on part of a song published in Robert Jones's *First Book of Songs and Airs* (1600). These popular songs would have seemed more distinct from the rest of the play for its early audiences. John Dover Wilson, in the 1930 Cambridge Shakespeare,

Table 1   *Twelfth Night*: A props table

Act/scene	Props needed
I.i	No formal props are required, apart from some source of music, which Orsino can command.
I.ii	Viola gives the Captain some money.
I.iii	No formal props are required.
I.iv	No formal props are required.
I.v	Olivia gives Viola some money, and her ring to Malvolio.
II.i	No formal props are required.
II.ii	Malvolio conveys Olivia's ring to Viola.
II.iii	No formal props required but, depending on how it is staged, drinking vessels may be used, Feste may have a musical instrument to accompany his song, and Malvolio may appear wearing his chain of office (lines 111–12).
II.iv	Orsino gives Cesario a jewel or a ring. There is some source of music, which Orsino can command. Depending on how it is staged, Feste may use a musical instrument to accompany his song.
II.v	A letter, which is placed for Malvolio to find, and 'a box tree' for three people to hide behind. This could easily be provided by a pillar, screen, or similar obstruction.
III.i	Feste may be playing music at the beginning of the scene. Cesario gives Feste two coins. We hear a clock striking.
III.ii	No formal props are required.
III.iii	Antonio gives Sebastian a purse of money.
III.iv	Malvolio appears in cross-gartered, yellow stockings. Sir Andrew appears with a letter. Olivia gives a jewel, containing her own miniature image in it, to Cesario. Sir Andrew, Cesario and Sir Toby all draw their swords. Cesario offers Antonio money.
IV.i	Sebastian gives Feste some money.
IV.ii	A gown and a false beard for Feste's Sir Topaz disguise.
IV.iii	Sebastian shows a pearl.
V.i	Feste has a letter. Orsino gives money to Feste. Malvolio has the letter he found in Act II, scene v. Depending on how it is staged, Feste may use a musical instrument to accompany his song.

rekindled a theory of F. G. Fleay, of 1876, that Shakespeare revised the text in Act II, scene iv. Viola intends to sing for Orsino (I.ii.54–5) and is called on to do so (II.iv.2–3). But Feste sings instead. The theory goes that the boy actor who played Viola could not sing (or not well enough), but that the necessary revision was not made consistently throughout the text. It is even possible that Shakespeare's first Viola could sing but when the play was later revived, Act II, scene iv was revised for the company's differently distributed talents.

Similarly, editorial practice over four hundred years has introduced emendations which may lose sight of the text as the early audiences might have seen and heard it. *Twelfth Night* first appeared in the Folio of 1623, the earliest attempt to collect all of Shakespeare's plays. There is no other early text. Did the play actually start with the music on which Orsino discourses (first inserted by Edward Capell in 1767–8), or was the music heard only when Orsino first called for it (I.i.1)? Did the early audiences see Maria take Sir Andrew's hand at I.iii.65, or are the editors of the Oxford edition (1994) interpolating stage business too readily there? Did the first audiences hear Sir Toby actually belch before cursing the pickled herring at I.v.115 (first inserted by Lewis Theobald in 1733), and does that mean that we do not hear him belch or break wind at any other point? Did Malvolio really exit on his powerful 'I'll be revenged on the whole pack of you' (V.i.378, inserted by Shakespeare's first critical editor Nicholas Rowe in 1709), even though no exit is marked in the Folio? And what colour were Sir Andrew Aguecheek's stockings? The Folio's 'dam'd colour'd' has encouraged editors to perceive a misreading of the manuscript from which the type was set. The New Variorum edition (1901) lists several different readings. Nicholas Rowe suggested 'flame-coloured' (1714), Charles Knight conjectured 'damask-coloured' (1840), and John Payne Collier 'dun-coloured' (1853). Other suggestions include 'damned-coloured' (Arden 2, 1975) and, perhaps most ingeniously, 'divers-coloured' (Oxford, 1994). In 1986, Barbara Everett suggested 'lemon-coloured', which would nicely prefigure Malvolio's yellow stockings. All of these could have a different impact on the portrayal of Sir Andrew in performance and on the humour of this particular moment. As a final example, Sir Toby, in the Folio, says on the approach of Maria 'Look where the youngest wren of mine comes'

(III.ii.63), which most editions (following Theobald in 1733) emend to 'nine'. The phrase is not proverbial, as far as we know, and Sir Toby's 'mine', though slightly unusual, makes good sense, especially given his later marriage to Maria. The emendation was explained in the eighteenth century by referring to the large number of eggs a wren produces, and by speculating about the diminutive stature of the boy actor who originally portrayed Maria.

Twelfth Night enjoyed popularity in the seventeenth century. There were performances at court for James I on Easter Monday 1618 and again at Candlemas 1623, when it was known as *Malvolio*. In Charles I's copy of the Second Folio (1632), he has written 'Malvolio' next to the play's title on the contents page as an aide-memoir. The popularity of the Malvolio plot is borne out by Leonard Digges (who died in 1636), in his commendatory verse at the front of a version of Shakespeare's *Poems* in 1640:

> Let but Beatrice
> And Benedick be seen, lo, in a trice
> The Cockpit galleries, boxes, all are full
> To hear Malvolio, that cross-gartered gull.
> ('Commendatory Poems and Prefaces',
> *The Oxford Shakespeare: The Complete Works*)

The popularity of the Malvolio plot continued into the eighteenth century. The earliest illustration of the play appeared in Nicholas Rowe's 1709 critical edition. Malvolio is shown in a darkened room, sitting on rushes. Next to him is a spilled bowl of food. A plump Feste as Sir Topaz, a thin Sir Toby and Maria smile and point on the other side of the door. The image owes nothing to Elizabethan stage practice.

Samuel Pepys saw forty-one performances of just twelve of Shakespeare's plays. He saw *Twelfth Night* three times. On 11 September 1661 he recorded:

> he [Dr Williams] and I walking through Lincoln's Inn fields, observed at the Opera a new play, *Twelfth Night*, was acted there, and the King [Charles II] there. So I, against my own mind and resolution, could not forbear to go in, which did make the play seem a burthen to me, and I took no pleasure at all

in it. And so after it was done, went home with my mind troubled for my
going thither, after swearing to my wife that I would never go to a play
without her.   (Latham and Mathews, vol. 2)

Pepys was clearly not in the mood that day, though he echoes Feste's
last song on leaving the theatre: 'that's all one, our play is *done*'. The
comic resolution of the wedding celebrations and reunions might
have been to blame for Pepys's reflections on his own marriage. He
saw the play and disliked it again on 6 January 1663: 'And after dinner
to the Duke's house and there saw *Twelfth Night* acted well, though it
be but a silly play and not relating at all to the name or day' (Latham
and Mathews, vol. 4). Pepys was not any more impressed when he
last recorded seeing it, on 20 January 1669:

and thence to the Duke of York's house and saw *Twelfth Night*, as it is now
revived, but I think one of the weakest plays that ever I saw on the stage.
So the play done, we home, my wife letting fall some words of her observing my eyes too mightily employed in the playhouse; meaning, upon
women, which did vex me; but however, when we came home we were
good friends; and so to read and to supper, and so to bed.   (Latham and
Mathews, vol. 9)

His phrase 'as it is now revived' suggests that Pepys saw the production starring Thomas Betterton as Sir Toby, Mr Loval as Malvolio and
Mrs Anne Gibbs as Viola. William Davenant, who used to claim he
was Shakespeare's illegitimate son, owned the exclusive rights to
produce *Twelfth Night* and nine other Shakespeare plays, which he
was happy 'to reform and make fit for the company of actors
appointed under his direction and command' (Wells, *Shakespeare: For
All Time*, p. 186). No one knows how far Davenant adapted *Twelfth
Night*, but it is likely that he titivated it to reflect Restoration taste.
Pepys obviously enjoyed the evening; both his and his wife's critical
glances might even have been sharpened through their own different
responses to the desire they saw portrayed in Shakespeare's play. It is
fortunate, though, that the posterity and reputation of *Twelfth Night*
does not rely on the greatest of diarists.

A century after Manningham's report, in 1703, William Burnaby's free adaptation *Love Betrayed, or The Agreeable Disappointment* burst onto the stage. Happily, it vanished just as suddenly. Only two performances of Burnaby's play are recorded over two years. Shakespeare's lines were chopped up and indiscriminately folded into inferior and sensational dialogue, which explains the sense of betrayal by Burnaby and the disappointment of his audiences. The first century of *Twelfth Night* drew to a close with a bout of distinctly unlicensed misrule.

The eighteenth century saw a major revival at the Theatre Royal, Drury Lane, in 1741. Charles Macklin played Malvolio and Hannah Pritchard played Viola. *Twelfth Night, or What You Will* has held the stage, delighting and moving audiences, ever since.

2 *Cultural Contexts and Sources*

There is no single, easily identifiable source for *Twelfth Night*. Instead, there are several texts whose influence on Shakespeare's work hovers at varying levels of suggestiveness. Three main contenders stand out as having significant bearing on Shakespeare's play: a popular Italian play *Gl'Ingannati* (1537), which Shakespeare might have known in one or more later adaptations in French, Spanish, Latin and Italian; Barnaby Riche's tale 'Apolonius and Silla' in *Riche His Farewell to Military Profession* (1581), perhaps the greatest single influence; and Emanual Forde's *The Famous History of Parismus* (1598). Extracts from these are reproduced below. All of them, together with other possible sources and analogues, are discussed in Geoffrey Bullough's *Narrative and Dramatic Sources of Shakespeare*, volume 2 (1958).

Material has been included which is not only most richly suggestive of episodes within Shakespeare's play, but which also shows how far Shakespeare's creative and alchemical process diverged from his background reading. A summary recommendation of other primary cultural sources then follows. A table with references to his other comedies suggests how *Twelfth Night* is sourced within Shakespeare's own oeuvre more generally. It is not the purpose of this section systematically to include all verbal allusions, or to give detailed plot summaries of the works referred to. Readers are encouraged to consult the sources themselves for these, as well as the critical material recommended in the 'Further Reading' section. Spelling has been modernized. Inevitable abridgements are signified by ellipses . . ., and any authorial insertions intended to clarify these are in italics thus: [*clarification*].

From Barnaby Riche's *Riche His Farewell to Military Profession* (1581)

Barnaby Riche (1542–1617) was an army captain who produced a volume of romantic stories. 'Apolonius and Silla' (the Orsino and Viola figures respectively) is set in Cyprus and Constantinople. Several moments which became episodes, or were alluded to, in *Twelfth Night* can be found, including the shipwreck, the disguise of Silla, the mistaken identity of Silvio (Sebastian, Silla's brother – very similar to each other in appearance, but not explicitly twins), and the comic resolution of the two marriages. Kenneth Muir notices in *Shakespeare's Sources* (1957) that four words used in 'Apolonius and Silla' are used by Shakespeare in *Twelfth Night*, but occur nowhere else in his work: 'coistrel', 'galliard', 'pavion' ('pavan'), and 'gaskins' (Muir, *Shakespeare's Sources*, p. 70).

The argument of the second history

Apolonius, duke, having spent a year's service in the wars against the Turk, returning homeward with his company by sea, was driven by force of weather to the isle of Cyprus, where he was well received by Pontus, governor of the same isle, with whom Silla, daughter to Pontus, fell so strangely in love that after Apolonius was departed to Constantinople, Silla, with one man followed, and coming to Constantinople, she served Apolonius in the habit of a man, and after many pretty accidents falling out, she was known to Apolonius, who, in requital of her love, married her.

. . . During the time that the famous city of Constantinople remained in the hands of the Christians, amongst many other noblemen that kept their abiding in that flourishing city was the one whose name was Apolonius, a worthy duke, who, being but a very young man, and even then new to his possessions, which were very great, levied a mighty band of men at his own proper charges with whom he served against the Turk during the space of one whole year. . . . When he had thus spent one year's service, he caused his trumpet to sound a retreat, and gathering his company together and embarking themselves, he set sail, holding his course towards Constantinople. But being upon the sea, by the extremity of the tempest which suddenly fell, his fleet was dissevered, some one way and some another; but he himself recovered the isle of Cyprus where he was worthily received by Pontus, duke and governor of the same isle, with whom he lodged while his ships were new repairing.

This Pontus that was lord and governor of this famous isle was an ancient duke and had two children, a son and a daughter. His son was named Silvio. . . .

The daughter her name was Silla, whose beauty was so peerless that she had the sovereignty amongst all other dames, as well for her beauty as for the nobleness of her birth. This Silla having heard of the worthiness of Apolonius, this young duke, who besides his beauty and good graces had a certain natural allurement, that being now in his company in her father's court, she was so strangely attached with the love of Apolonius, that there was nothing might content her but his presence and sweet sight . . . she strived with herself to leave her fondness, but all in vain. . . .

[*Apolonius returns to Constantinople. Silla decides to go after him, accompanied by her servant, Pedro. There is a storm at sea.*]

This storm continued all that day and the next night, and they [. . .] were driven upon the main shore, where the galley broke all to pieces. There was every man providing to save his own life: some got upon hatches, boards, and casks, and were driven with the waves to and fro; but the greatest number were drowned, amongst the which Pedro was one. But Silla herself being in the cabin [. . .] took hold of a chest that was the captain's, the which, by the only providence of God brought her safe to the shore, the which when she had recovered, not knowing what was become of Pedro her man, she deemed that both he and all the rest had been drowned for that she saw nobody upon the shore but herself. Wherefore, when she had awhile made great lamentations, complaining her mishaps, she began in the end to comfort herself with the hope that she had to see her Apolonius, and found such means that she brake open the chest, that brought her to land, wherein she found good store of coin, and sundry suits of apparel that were the captain's. And now, to prevent a number of injuries that might be proffered to a woman that was left in her case, she determined to leave her own apparel and sort herself into some of those suits, that, being taken for a man, she might pass through the country in the better safety. And as she changed her apparel, she thought it likewise convenient to change her name, wherefore, not readily happening of any other, she called herself Silvio, by the name of her own brother whom you have heard spoken of before.

In this manner she travelled to Constantinople, where she inquired out the palace of the Duke of Apolonius, and thinking herself now to be fit and able to play the servingman, she presented herself to the duke, craving his service. The duke, very willing to give succour unto strangers, perceiving him to be a proper smug young man, gave him entertainment. Silla . . . above the rest of his servants was very diligent and attendant upon him, the which the duke perceiving, began likewise to grow into good liking with the diligence of his man, and therefore made him one of his chamber. Who but Silvio then was most near about him, in helping of him to make him ready in a morning, in the setting of his ruffs, in the keeping of his chamber? Silvio pleased his master so well that above all the rest of his servants about him, he had the greatest credit, and the duke put him most in trust.

At this very instant there was remaining in the city a noble dame, a widow, whose husband was but lately deceased, one of the noblest men that were in the parts of Grecia, who left his lady and wife large posses- sions and great livings. This lady's name was called Julina, who, besides the abundance of her wealth and the greatness of her revenues, had like- wise the sovereignty of all the dames of Constantinople for her beauty. To this lady Julina Apolonius became an earnest suitor, and according to the manner of wooers, besides fair words, sorrowful sighs, and piteous coun- tenances, there must be sending of loving letters, chains, bracelets, brooches, rings, tablets, gems, jewels, and presents – I know not what. [. . .] And who must be the messenger . . . but Silvio his man, in him the duke reposed his only confidence to go between him and his lady.

Now gentlewomen, do you think there could have been a greater torment devised wherewith to afflict the heart of Silla, than herself to be made the instrument to work her own mishap and to play the attorney in a cause that made so much against herself? But Silla, altogether desirous to please her master, cared nothing at all to offend herself, followed his business with so good a will as if it had been in her own preferment.

Julina, now having many times taken the gaze of this young youth Silvio, perceiving him to be of such excellent perfect grace, was so entan- gled with the often sight of this sweet temptation that she fell into as great a liking with the man as the master was with herself.

[. . . Silvio loved] his sister as dearly as his own life, and the rather for that as she was his natural sister, both by father and mother, so the one of them was so like the other in countenance and favour that there was no man able to discern one from the other by their faces, saving by their apparel, the one being a man, the other a woman.

Silvio therefore, vowed to his father not only to seek out his sister Silla, but also to revenge the villainy which he conceived in Pedro for carrying away of his sister. [. . .] At the last he arrived in Constantinople, where, as he was walking in an evening for his own recreation on a pleasant green yard without the walls of the city, he fortuned to meet with the lady Julina, who likewise had been abroad to take the air. And as she suddenly cast her eyes upon Silvio, thinking him to be her old acquaintance . . . said unto him:

'Sir Silvio, if your haste be not the greater, I pray you let me have a little talk with you, seeing I have so luckily met you in this place. . . . Considering how many noble men there hath been here before, and be yet at this present, which hath both served, sued, and most humbly entreated to attain to that which to you of myself I have freely offered, and I perceive is despised or at least very lightly regarded.'

Silvio, wondering at these words, but more amazed that she could so rightly call him by his name, could not tell what to make of her speeches, assuring himself that she was deceived and did mistake him, did think, notwithstanding, it had been a point of great simplicity if he should forsake that which fortune had so favourably proffered unto him, perceiving by her train that she was some lady of great honour . . . answered thus:

'Madam, if before this time I seemed to forget myself in neglecting your courtesy which so liberally you have meant unto me, please it you to pardon what is past, and from this day forwards Silvio remaineth ready . . . to make such reasonable amends as his ability may any ways permit, or as it shall please you to command.'

Julina, the gladdest woman that might be to hear these joyful news, said:

'Then, my Silvio, see you fail not tomorrow at night to sup with me at my own house where I will discourse further with you what amends you shall make me.'

[*Silvio finds out more about Julina from a passer-by. Both Silvio and Julina spend the night and following day in a state of great excitement until supper time arrives. After supper, Julina asks Silvio to stay with her for the night. She becomes pregnant by him. Silvio leaves and decides never to return to her, and resumes his search for Silla.*]

The Duke Apolonius, having made a long suit . . . came to Julina to crave her direct answer. . . .

Julina . . . was at a controversy in herself what she might do . . . did think it therefore best to conceal the matter till she might speak with Silvio to use his opinion how these matters should be handled.

[*The duke hears about his servant Silvio's affair with Julina. Silvio begs him to* wait and not to judge until there is definite proof. He promises to confess all – even to be put to death – if what the duke suspects is true. The duke refuses to be persuaded. Julina wonders why Silvio has stayed away from her; her pregnancy begins to show, and she learns that Silvio is in prison. Julina begs Apolonius to release Silvio. Silvio denies her suit and Julina explains that she is pregnant by him. Silvio publicly doubts her and begins to shame her with charges of filthiness. Julina's further protestations move the duke to pity, who demands that Silvio make good his claims, or be put to death. Julina and Silvio retire to talk in private.]

[Silvio], loosing his garments down to his stomach, and showed Julina his breasts and pretty teats surmounting far the whiteness of snow itself, saying: 'Lo, madam! Behold here the party whom you have challenged to be the father of your child. See, I am a woman, the daughter of a noble duke, who only for the love of him whom you so lightly have shaken off, have forsaken my father, abandoned my country, and in manner as you see, am become a servingman, satisfying myself but with the only sight of my Apolonius. And now madam, if my passion were not vehement, and my torments without comparison, I would wish that my feigned griefs might be laughed to scorn and my dissembled pains to be rewarded with flouts. But my love being pure, my travail continual, and my griefs endless, I trust madam, you will not only excuse me of crime but also pity my distress, the which I protest, I would still have kept secret if my fortune would have so permitted.'

[Julina now feels worse than ever since she does not know who is the father of her child. She explains what has happened to the duke and goes home in shame and despondency.]

But the duke, more amazed to hear this strange discourse of Silvio, came unto him, whom, when he viewed with better consideration, perceived indeed that it was Silla the daughter of Duke Pontus, and embracing her in his arms said:

'O the branch of all virtue and the flower of courtesy itself! Pardon me, I beseech you, of all the discourtesies as I have ignorantly committed towards you, desiring you that without further memory of ancient griefs you will accept of me, who is more joyful and better contented with your presence, than if the whole world were at my commandment.'

. . . He provided for her sundry suits of sumptuous apparel, and the marriage day appointed, which was celebrated with great triumph through the whole city of Constantinople. . . .

[The news spreads all over Greece and Silvio hears about it.]

He, being the gladdest man in the world, hastened to Constantinople, where coming to his sister he was joyfully received and most lovingly welcomed and entertained of the duke his brother-in-law. After he had remained there two or three days, the duke revealed unto Silvio the whole discourse how it happened between his sister and the Lady Julina, and how his sister was challenged for getting a woman with child. Silvio, blushing with these words, was stricken with great remorse to make Julina amends. . . . He therefore betrayed the whole circumstance to the duke, whereof the duke being very joyful, immediately repaired with Silvio to the house of Julina. . . .

Julina, seeing Silvio in place, did know very well that he was the father of her child, and was so ravished with joy that she knew not whether she were awake or in some dream. Silvio, embracing her in his arms, craving forgiveness of all that was passed, concluded with her the marriage day, which was presently accomplished with great joy and contentation to all parties. And thus Silvio, having attained a noble wife and Silla, his sister, her desired husband, they passed the residue of their days with such delight as those that have accomplished the perfection of their felicities.

Gl'Ingannati, 'The Deceived', Anonymous, 1537

First produced by a literary society in Siena, this comedy has much in common with several subsequent European versions, in which a girl disguised as a boy falls in love with her master. The Feast of the Epiphany ('la notte di Beffana') is mentioned explicitly in its prologue as well as being referred to in Act I, scene ii, and might have helped Shakespeare choose the first of his two titles. The plot is almost impenetrable in its intricacies. Lelia (Viola) is in love with Flamminio (Orsino), who loves Isabella (Olivia), who loves Lelia (disguised as Fabio: Cesario). Isabella's father, Gherardo, and his servant Spela are reminiscent of Sir Toby and Sir Andrew; Clemenzia the nurse (and sometime mistress of Virginio, Lelia's aged father) and Pasquella (maid to Gherardo) are similar to Maria. Lelia's older brother Fabrizio (Sebastian) is mistaken for Fabio and eventually marries Isabella. Flamminio believes himself betrayed by Lelia, but marries her on discovering her true love for him. *Gl'Ingannati* is a farce entirely in prose, and the creative powers with which Shakespeare transformed its prosaic, situational comedy are pervasive throughout any reading of it.

These extracts, freshly translated into modern English by Tom Matheson and Angela Cutrale, are based on an Italian facsimile edition of *Gl'Ingannati con Il Sacrificio e La Canzone nella Morte d'una Civetta* (dated 1537, published by the Accademici Intronati di Siena). This is a free translation not in the sense of altering or distorting the original, but in substituting modern English words, word-order, phrases and grammatical construction – particularly shorter separate sentences instead of prolonged comma-separated clauses – for the old Italian. Previous English translations of *Gl'Ingannati*, in Geoffrey Bullough's *Narrative and Dramatic Sources of Shakespeare* (1958) and Bruce Penman's *Five Italian Renaissance Comedies* (1978), have been consulted, but not reproduced.

From Act I, scene iii

LELIA   When I think of it, knowing the bad habits of the young men in Modena, it's very reckless of me to go out alone at this hour. It would serve me right if one of them took me by force into some nearby house to see if I was actually a man or a woman. That would teach me to go out so early. But the reason is the love I feel for Flamminio, ungrateful and indifferent as he is. What a terrible destiny! I love someone who hates me, who despises me. I serve someone who doesn't even recognise me. Even worse, I'm helping him make love to someone else – if they knew it, no one would believe it. And all without any hope, except seeing him all day, with my own eyes. So far everything's gone well enough, but how will I manage now? What can I do next? My father's come back. Flamminio has come to live in town. I can't stay here without being recognised. And if that happens I'll be condemned for ever. I'll be a laughing-stock in the whole town. . . .

CLEMENZIA   What's the use of this madness?

LELIA   What use? Do you realise how unhappy it makes a woman in love to see her lover, to speak to him, touch him . . . to be sure that if she can't have him, no else will?

CLEMENZIA   This is lunacy. You're only throwing wood on the fire, if you're not sure that this will please your lover. How do you serve him?

LELIA   At the table, in his room. And I know I've pleased him so much in these two weeks that if I'd only done it as my real self – as a woman – I'd be truly happy.

CLEMENZIA   Tell me. Where do you sleep?

LELIA   In the next room, alone.

CLEMENZIA   And what would happen if one night he's tempted to call you in to sleep with him?

LELIA   I don't want to think of difficulties before I come to them. If such a thing happened, I'd think about it, and decide.

LELIA   I'll tell you. Flamminio, as I've already said, is in love with Isabella Foiani and he often sends me to her with letters and messages. She thinks I'm a boy and has fallen madly in love with me, and treats me with the greatest affection in the world. I pretend that I can't love her until Flamminio himself stops loving her. I think I've brought everything to a head, and I hope that, within three or four days, it will be all over, and he'll give her up.

From Act I, scene iv

CLEMENZIA   I want to lead him on a bit. Good morning Gherardo, God give you good day. This morning you look just like a cherub.

GHERARDO   May God give you a hundred thousand ducats, and more.

SPELA   They would suit me better.

GHERARDO   Oh Spela, how happy I'd be if I could be her.

SPELA   Why? So you could have tried as many husbands, instead of trying just one wife? Or are you thinking of something else?

CLEMENZIA   And how many husbands am I supposed to have had, Spela? God curse you with flies. Are you sure you're not jealous that you weren't one of them?

SPELA   Yes, by God. Pleasure's always welcome.

GHERARDO   Be quiet, animal. I'm not saying it for that.

SPELA   Why are you saying it then?

GHERARDO   Because I would have hugged, kissed, and cuddled my Lelia – sweet with sugar, with gold, with milk, with roses – with I don't know what.

SPELA   Oh Master, let's go home, at once!

From Act II, scene i

FLAMMINIO   Please tell me again, Fabio, what she said yesterday evening when you took my letter.

LELIA   I've told you already, twenty times.

FLAMMINIO   Tell me once again. What does it matter to you?

LELIA   It does matter. It matters because I can see it makes you unhappy. And that makes me as unhappy as you. As your servant, I only want to please you, and if I give you her reply, you will blame me.

FLAMMINIO   Don't be afraid, my Fabio. I love you as a brother. I know you love me and you can be sure I'll never let you down. As time will show, God willing. Rely on that. But what did she say? . . .

LELIA   Tell me. Don't you have anyone in this town who'd actually want your love?

FLAMMINIO   Yes, I do. Among others, there's one called Lelia. I've wanted to say a thousand times that she looks just like you. The most beautiful, intelligent, graceful young person in this town. As I hope to show you one day.

LELIA   If this poor young woman was your first, and still loves you more than ever, why have you left her for someone else? That's a sin God might not forgive. Oh Signor Flamminio, you do her wrong.

FLAMMINIO   You're still just a child, Fabio. You can't know the power of love. I can tell you I'm compelled to love this other woman. I adore her and I know I can't, and I won't, think of anyone but her. So go back and speak to her again, and get from her own mouth what she has against me, why she doesn't want to see me.

LELIA   You're wasting your time.

FLAMMINIO   I'm glad to waste my time.

LELIA   You won't achieve anything.

FLAMMINIO   So be it.

From Act II, scene vi

[*There is no Malvolio figure in the play, though there is reference to 'per il mal ch'io vi voglio' – 'for the ill-will I bear you' – in the Prologue. There is also an eavesdropping scene. Crivello, the servant of Flamminio and Scatizza, the servant of Virginio, overhear Lelia and Isabella.*]

ISABELLA   Listen for a moment.

LELIA   Here I am.

ISABELLA   Is there anyone outside?

LELIA   Not a living creature.
    (CRIVELLO   What the devil does she want?)
    (SCATIZZA   This intimacy is too much!)
    (CRIVELLO   Wait and see.)
ISABELLA   Just another word.
    (CRIVELLO   They're getting too close.)
    (SCATIZZA   They are. They are.)
ISABELLA   YOU know, I want . . .
LELIA   What do you want?
ISABELLA   I would like you . . . to come closer.
    (SCATIZZA   Come closer, you little savage.)
ISABELLA   Make sure there's no-one there.

    (SCATIZZA   Kiss her, unless you want the plague.)
    (CRIVELLO   She's still afraid of being seen.)
LELIA   Come on, go back inside.
ISABELLA   I want a favour from you.
LELIA   What favour?
ISABELLA   Come inside the doorway.
    (SCATIZZA   The thing is done.)
ISABELLA   Oh, you are cruel!
LELIA   Someone will see us.
    (CRIVELLO   Oh dear, Oh dear! How cross this makes me!)
    (SCATIZZA   Didn't I tell you he would kiss her?)
    (CRIVELLO   I can tell you I'd rather not have seen that kiss than win a
    hundred scudi.)

From Act II, scene vii

[*Flamminio declares to Fabio that he will convince Isabella that he no longer
loves Lelia. Fabio faints.*]

FLAMMINIO   Give me your arm. You're frozen. Now go very slowly.
    How strange is man's life? I wouldn't lose this boy for everything I
    own. I don't know if there's ever been a cleverer, more courtly
    servant in the world than this young boy. And, more than that, he
    seems to love me so much that if he were a woman I would think
    him *sick* with love.

From Act III, scene i

[Fabrizio and his servant Stragualcia arrive in Modena. A pedant advises them on the sights, calling to mind Sebastian and Antonio in III. iii. of Twelfth Night.]

PEDANT   You'll see here the most imposing campanile there is in the whole world.

STRAGUALCIA   Is that the one the Modenesi wanted to make a sheath for? The one whose shadow is supposed to make men mad?

PEDANT   Yes, that's the one.

STRAGUALCIA   Whoever wants to see it, let him. Now let's look for somewhere to stay. I know I'll never come out of the kitchen.

PEDANT   You're in a great hurry.

STRAGUALCIA   Dammit, I'm dying of hunger. I've eaten nothing this morning except half a chicken that was in the boat.

FABRIZIO   Let's find someone who can take us to my father's house.

PEDANT   No, it seems to me that we should first find an inn, and settle in there. And then, at leisure, find your father.

FABRIZIO   That's fine. These must be the inns.

From Act III, scene v

FABRIZIO   Madam, you don't know me. Please go away. You've mistaken me for someone else.

PASQUELLA   Don't be offended, my Fabio. I'm only saying it for your own good.

FABRIZIO   I'm not offended. But it's not my name. And I'm not who you take me for.

PASQUELLA   Have it your own way. But realise, young man, there aren't many girls as rich and as beautiful in this town. And I wish you'd give up what you're doing, going backwards and forwards every day, taking and bringing back messages, making people talk, with no benefit to you, and no honour to her.

FABRIZIO   This is something new I don't understand. Either she's mad, or she's mistaken me for someone else. I'll go where she wants to take me. Let's go.

From Act V, scene iii

CLEMENZIA   This is your Fabio, Signor Flamminio. Look at him well. Do

you know him? You seem surprised. And can you see in this girl the
faithful and constant lover I told you about? Look at her well, to see if
you recognise her or not. Have you lost your tongue? What does that
mean? And you are the one who so little appreciated the love of your
own lady. This is the truth. You're not deceived. You know I'm telling
the truth . . .

FLAMMINIO   I don't believe there could ever be a better trick than this in
the world . Have I been so blind that I never once recognized her?

LELIA   Flamminio, you're my lord. You know what I've done and for
whom I did it. I have no other wish than this.

FLAMMINIO   You have certainly proved it. Forgive me if I've made you
unhappy, without recognising you. I am utterly penitent and admit
my mistake.

LELIA   You could never do anything more to make me happy, Signor
Flamminio.

FLAMMINIO   Clemenzia, I don't want to wait any longer, in case some
accident disturbs our good fortune. I want to marry her straight away,
if she's content.

LELIA   As content as could be!

The Famous History of Parismus, by Emanuel Forde (1598)

This novel may have provided Shakespeare with the names of two of
his characters: Parismus is in love with Laurana, daughter of the King
and Queen of Thessaly. Her mother's name is Olivia. Violetta also
falls in love with Parismus, and Pollipus falls in love with Violetta;
Parismus woos her on behalf of Pollipus, but she won't be won.
Instead, she disguises herself as a page in order to follow Parismus.
The writing is explicit in its eroticism, which, although different and
apparently more restrained in Shakespeare's play, can become highly
charged in performances.

From Chapter 17

Pollipus still earnestly prosecuted his suit unto Violetta, who hearing that
Parismus was departing towards his own country, determined to venture
her life and credit to go with him, and therefore fitted herself in page's
apparel, which so well became her, that she seemed to be the artificialest

workmanship that ever nature had framed, her suit being green satin, her buskins of the finest Spanish leather, fastened to her dainty leg with crystal buttons, her hair wreathed with a carnation ribbon, and all things else so neat and so comely upon her delicate body . . . she secretly stole from her father's house . . . she was not in that habit any way suspected . . . she laboured by all means to be entertained by Parismus.

And on a time espying him with Laurana, walking privately in the garden, on a sudden she came towards them, who beholding her comely shape and delicate complexion, deemed her rather to be a divine than a mortal creature. . . . Parismus demanded whose page he was.

'My lords,' said Violetta, 'as yet I have no master, but I would gladly be entertained.'

Quoth he then, 'Would you attend on Laurana and myself, if it please her to like you?'

'I am,' quoth she, 'in all humble duty ready at your command.'

Many questions Laurana asked the boy (as she supposed) demanding his name, his country and parentage.

Violetta answered, 'My name is Adonius, my country Greece, and my parents all dead'. . . . Which speeches poor Violetta uttered with so pretty a grace, that they both took great delight in her behaviour. . . .

From Chapter 20

[*In their travels, Parismus, Pollipus and Adonius meet a Hermit and stay the night with him. The three of them share a bed.*]

And for that Adonius was somewhat sickly, they laid him in the midst betwixt them, for that he had done them many pleasures in their travel, Parismus being so far in love with him, as he would have ventured his own life for to do him good. Poor Adonius with blushing cheeks put off his apparel, and seemed to be abashed when he was in his shirt, and tenderly leapt into the bed betwixt these two worthy knights, who little suspected that it was Violetta, where the poor soul lay close at Parismus's back, the very sweet touch of whose body seemed to ravish her with joy: and on the other side not acquainted with such bedfellows, she seemed (as it were) metamorphosed, with a kind of delightful fear. But had Pollipus known it had been his dear Violetta, he would have more kindly regarded his bedfellow, who seemed to start if Pollipus did but stir. Thus they all took their rest for that night, the two knights only being glad of this quiet repose after long travail; Adonius having in his heart a thousand delights of joy by touching Parismus's sweet body. . . .

From Chapter 24

[*Once Parismus and Laurana have been reunited, Violetta begins to love Pollipus, but she is still in disguise.*]

Violetta's joys were as exceeding as his sorrows were extreme, for she continually beheld the constancy that reigned in his heart to herwards [*i.e. towards her*], the noble gifts wherewith his mind was endued, the comeliness of his goodly proportion, which might well please a curious lady's eye, his unconquered valour and prowess, wherewith he achieved incredible victories with great fame, the friendship and courteous behaviour that abundantly flowed from his gentle heart, whereby it was apparent that he did not disdain the meanest persons . . . , and also the pleasure she took in his company, being never from him in the daytime, and his bedfellow in the night, that she was privy to all his actions, using many kindnesses, which he full little thought proceeded from such affection. And nothing deeming Violetta had been so privy to all his cogitations, though she, poor soul, never touched his body, but with trembling fear, remembering her own nakedness, still using such bashfulness in her actions, as if many eyes had been privy to her disguise, and watchfully noted her behaviour, wherewith her joys continued in such secret content.

From Chapter 29

[*Violetta removes her disguise and she and Pollipus are united.*]

Violetta was ashamed to utter her mind in that place, but being sure he could not behold her blushing cheeks said, 'The request that I make is this: that you will give me your faithful promise, that at such time as it is your hap to meet Violetta, and obtain her good will, that the first night you will not offer to do anything, that may tend to her dishonour.'

'Upon mine honour,' said Pollipus, 'I will not do anything whatsoever, disagreeable to her will, for so dear do I esteem her, that I would rather destroy myself, than she should be any way displeased with me.'

'Then know, worthy knight,' quoth she, 'I am that Violetta you so earnestly enquire after. I am the party that have so long time procured your discontent, and I am she whose absence you have so oft bewailed, and now I am constrained to manifest myself unto you, desiring you to pardon my hardheartedness that have so long concealed myself, and thereby procured your disquiet.'

Pollipus, hearing her speeches, could not tell what to say. . . . At last he said, 'I know not what to conjecture, nor how to behave myself, nor whether I should call you Adonius or Violetta, considering how unlikely it is she should be so kind to me, and how certain I am that Adonius hath done me manifold pleasures. Then, sweet Violetta, if you are she, resolve me of this my doubt, being thereby driven to that hopeful despair, that I know not whether my fortune be better or worse than it was.'

Violetta thinking a little back said, 'Pardon me, dear Pollipus, for I am your unworthy friend Violetta that have, in this disguise, made trial of my fortune and your friendship.'

Pollipus then took her most lovingly in his arms, not offering other than his former promise did permit. Yet he was in a doubt still and could not be quiet until he had used such kind means (yet far from dishonour) as thereby he found she was a virgin, and no page, and therefore assured himself it was Violetta. And, folding her delicate and tender body in his manlike arms (which he had oftentimes before embraced, but not with such kindness, banishing all sadness from his sorrowful heart) with sweet and delightful content he embraced her with that kindness that long parted lovers enjoy when they so pleasantly meet, spending the rest of the night in pleasing and delightful communication, and remembrances of their former kindnesses, which augmented their joys to an exceeding height.

Shakespeare's earlier comedies

Table 2 draws together major points of comparison between *Twelfth Night* and some of Shakespeare's other comedies which preceded it. It is far from being exhaustive, but suggests an overview of how the play is sourced within Shakespeare's own wider creative output and developing theatrical interests within a particular genre. References to the comparable work come first, with points of correspondence to *Twelfth Night* following in brackets.

Other cultural influences

The development in literary criticism of New Historicism and Cultural Materialism from the early 1980s has encouraged the practice of locating Shakespeare's plays in the context of social, political,

Table 2 Shakespeare as source for *Twelfth Night*

Shakespearian comedy	Comparison to *Twelfth Night, or What You Will*
The Two Gentlemen of Verona (late 1580s)	I.i.65–9 Proteus declares himself sick in love (cf. Orsino, I.i.1–15).
	I.i.105–30 Julia's having to make sense of scraps of a letter; Valentine tricked by a letter II.i.97–161 (cf. Malvolio II.v.82–168).
	II.vii.40–90 Julia decides to disguise herself as a page and find Proteus (cf. Viola I.ii.44–61).
	III.ii.51–97 Proteus advises Sir Thurio how to woo Silvia; and V.ii.1–50 tells him what she thinks (cf. Sir Toby, Sir Andrew, Fabian and Viola III.ii.1–61; III.iv.137–93; III.iv.211–300).
	IV.ii.53–73 Julia's melancholic responses to the love song (cf. Viola II.iv.13.1–40).
	IV.iv.39–202 Proteus sends Julia as Sebastian to Silvia on a love errand; Silvia and Julia meet; Julia soliloquizes (cf. Orsino, Viola, Olivia I.iv.12–42; I.v.160–278; II.ii.17–41; II.iv.78–124; III.i.82–162).
	V.ii.145–75 Julia projects herself into an imaginary account of Proteus's love (cf. Viola II.iv.107–22).
	V.iv.84–119 Proteus and Julia are reunited (cf. Viola and Orsino V.i.258–267).
The Comedy of Errors (1594)	I.i.28–139 Two sets of identical male twins separated by a shipwreck (cf. I.ii.1–15).
	I.ii.9–16 One twin asks to meet his servant in an inn after some sightseeing (cf. Sebastian and Antonio III.iii.).
	I.ii.33–40 One twin's yearning for another (cf. II.i.15–28; III.iv.364–75).
	II.i.84–114 Self-pity and worry of Adriana (cf. Olivia III.i.109–62; III.iv.194–210).
	V.i.332–430 Reunion of twins (cf. V.i.202–62).

Shakespearian comedy	Comparison to *Twelfth Night, or What You Will*
Love's Labour's Lost (1594)	I.i.1–32 Idealism of King, Longueville and Dumaine about three-year fast (cf. Orsino's idealism and Olivia's seven-year fast I.i.1–40). IV.i.59–86; IV.ii.89–144; IV.iii.187–226 Confusion over wrongly delivered love letters (cf. Malvolio's letter V.i.278–346). IV.iii.1–173 A virtuoso eavesdropping scene of young men composing love poems (cf. Malvolio being overheard II.v.13–197). V.ii.13–28 Catherine tells of her sister dying of melancholy in love (cf. Viola II.iv.105–22).
The Merchant of Venice (1596/7)	I.i.113–85; IV.i.5–12, 261–84 Extreme loyalty of Antonio for his friend Bassanio (cf. Antonio and Sebastian II.i; III.iv.299–363; V.i.54–91).
The Merry Wives of Windsor (1597?)	I.i.181, 263–79 Abraham Slender's naivety, clottishness, wistful expressions and inter-actions with Anne Page (cf. Sir Andrew Aguecheek I.iii.41–75; II.iii.18–24; V.i.168–87). II.i.1–96 Falstaff's love letters mocked by Mistresses Page and Ford and revenge agreed on (cf. Malvolio tricked with love letter and promising revenge V.i.368).
Much Ado About Nothing (1598–9)	II.iii.35–232; III.i.15–116 Benedick and Beatrice gulled into love in eavesdropping scenes (cf. Malvolio II.v.13–197).

philosophical, religious, scientific, economic, and conduct literature, and of the works of art of their period, both plays by other authors and works of fiction, poetry, paintings, monuments, music, and so forth. Such exploration has succeeded in broadening the field of literary studies not only to consider the production of a single literary work by a single artist, but to consider how culture itself is produced,

disseminated, and ordered. Having provided a generous selection
from the literary sources that Shakespeare used in writing *Twelfth
Night*, the scope of a *Handbook* allows only a few recommendations of
other works, texts, and areas which the reader may wish to consult
and explore in pursuit of these inexhaustible questions. Such a
pursuit is inexhaustible *and* limitless because a selection of any representative body of primary, contemporary work which may be
considered in relation to *Twelfth Night* could just as well be made
because of its relevance to *all* of Shakespeare's other works, to those
of his contemporaries, and to their life, and cultural experiences of
the world. There are, of course, certain works and testimony from
Shakespeare's time which deserve special consideration and the
Bibliography gives details of books that consider and reproduce
some of them. Bruce R. Smith's source book *Twelfth Night or What You
Will: Texts and Contexts* (2001) and Leslie Hotson's imaginative *The First
Night of 'Twelfth Night'* (1954) may be of particular interest from this
point of view.

For a reader wishing to immerse himself or herself more into the
world out of which *Twelfth Night* arose, the following Elizabethan and
Jacobean writings would be good places to start. John Manningham's
diary (1602–3; edited by Robert Parker Sorlien) provides wonderful
eye-witness accounts of his social world. Philip Stubbes's puritan
polemic *The Anatomie of Abuses in Ailgna* (1583; edited by Margaret Jane
Kidnie) would shine a Malvolio-style light onto theatres and social
debauchery; Thomas Heywood's *An Apology for Actors* (1612) would
help to balance Stubbes's puritanical attack. Michel de Montaigne's
essay 'On Friendship' (which is widely available) provides a context
for understanding the relationship between Orsino and Cesario,
Antonio and Sebastian. The music of John Dowland and Thomas
Morley gives an impression of what the songs in the play might have
sounded like (James Walker's editions of the settings appear in an
appendix to the Oxford edition). Dipping into *The Penguin Book of
Renaissance Verse* (edited by Henry Woudhuysen) and *The New Oxford
Book of Sixteenth-Century Verse* (edited by Emrys Jones) would help to
flesh out the lyrical context of the play (Shakespeare's own Sonnets 1,
3, 8, 9 and 11 – all about procreation – and 134, 135, 136 and 143 –
punning on 'Will' – have particular resonance in relation to *Twelfth*

Night, Or What You Will). A contemporary portrait showing what fools looked like, *We Three*, is reproduced in the Oxford edition and hangs in the exhibition of Shakespeare's life and times in the Birthplace at Stratford-upon-Avon (log on to www.shakespeare. org.uk). A visit to an Elizabethan manor house would convey an impression of the social sphere of Olivia; a palace (such as Hampton Court) would convey Orsino's (log on to www.hrp.org.uk). The Middle Temple on the Strand in London is evocative of how the play was staged there; Shakespeare's Globe (and the accompanying exhibition) on Bankside also evokes how it was staged (log on to www.shakespearesglobe.org.uk). Finally, a visit to the Tudor galleries in the National Portrait Gallery in London to see the full-size pictures and the exquisite miniatures would help to convey how people looked, dressed, and wanted to be known (log on to www.npg.org.uk). All the websites recommended provide the opportunity to find out more and see visual images.

3 Key Productions and Performances

There now follow four separate accounts of important productions, all of which attempt to convey a sense of what the performances were like, as well as how they were received by their contemporary audiences. Readers are invited to make connections between the accounts as they read; the many inevitable echoes of theatre history will no doubt become even more apparent as these productions are conjured up and re-imagined afresh. Of the four, the only production seen by the author is the 2005 Royal Shakespeare Company production, directed by Michael Boyd.

The Lyceum Theatre, London, 1884

The evening of 8 July 1884 was impossibly warm, and the Lyceum was packed to capacity. The much heralded revival of *Twelfth Night* seemed, as the evening wore on, not only to have promised more than it was delivering, but fundamentally to disappoint Sir Henry Irving's many enthusiastic admirers. When the curtain came down there arose enough booing and hissing for the great actor manager to make the following speech:

> I can't understand how a company of earnest comedians and admirable actors, having these three cardinal virtues of actors – being sober, clean, and perfect – and having exercised their abilities on one of the most difficult plays, can have given any cause for dissatisfaction. (Pemberton, *Ellen Terry*, p. 253)

Pemberton thought that 'why it failed to please the audience was a mystery that remains unsolved' (p. 252). Theatre criticism has since unravelled the puzzle, if not penetrated the heart of it.

On balance, it appears to have had every chance of success: the lavishness of visual style that had become the woof and warp of Irving's success at the Lyceum (he had been in charge of it since 1878) – twelve beautifully drawn backdrops shown over fifteen scenes – and one of the greatest theatrical partnerships of all time: the extraordinary Sir Henry Irving himself and Dame Ellen Terry. They had appeared opposite each other as Hamlet and Ophelia, Portia and Shylock, Richard III and Lady Anne, Romeo and Juliet, and Beatrice and Benedick by the time they came to play Malvolio and Viola.

Irving had a highly distinctive way of moving and speaking which divided his critics. Edward Gordon Craig (son of Ellen Terry) offers a defence of Irving in his 1930 critical biography. He attempts to describe how Irving spoke and moved, and the effect this had on stage. 'He would say "Gud" for "God"; "Cut-thrut dug" for "Cut throat dog" (Shylock); "Tack the rup frum mey neck" for "Take the rope from my neck" (Mathias in *The Bells*)' (Craig, *Henry Irving*, p. 62). From Craig's observations, it is possible to imagine how Irving might have spoken the line 'some are born great, some achieve greatness, and some have greatness thrust upon 'em' (II.v.135–7): 'Sum arr boyrner greyt, sum arrcheever greytnesser, ond sum harver greytenesser thrubst uborn 'eym.' For Craig, Irving's way of speaking enriched the language, finding in its vowel sounds a transhistorical undercurrent of an earthy and wholesome medievalism. Irving's way of walking was often mocked by cartoonists: hopelessly gangly, wiry, bent legs, bent knees and dragging feet. Craig explains that 'the ordinary life was being put away; something was coming into his blood [. . .] he danced, he did not merely walk – he sang, he by no means merely spoke. He was essentially artificial in distinction to being merely natural' (Craig, *Henry Irving*, pp. 73–4). For Irving's dissenters, the artifice was always of too similar a kind. George Bernard Shaw found Irving sadly lacking as an interpretative actor: 'The truth is that he has never in his life conceived or interpreted the characters of any author except himself' (Shaw, reviewing *Cymbeline*, in *Shaw on Shakespeare*, p. 53). Ellen Terry captures a passing moment of self-revelation in her autobiography:

Once when I was touring with him in America, at the time when he was at the highest point of his fame, I watched him one day in the train – always a delightful occupation, for his face provided many pictures in a minute – and being struck by a curious look, half puzzled, half despairing, asked him what he was thinking about.

'I was thinking,' he answered slowly, 'how strange it is that I should have made the reputation I have as an actor, with nothing to help me – with no equipment. My legs, my voice – everything has been against me. For an actor who can't walk, can't talk, and has no face to speak of, I've done pretty well.'   (quoted in Craig, *Henry Irving*, pp. 68–9)

Ellen Terry was far less controversial in the fame she courted, being almost universally adored for her natural charm, grace of demeanour, and resonant humour. She could enter a room of people and within seconds collective laughter would follow her as she moved around it. 'When she spoke,' wrote Virginia Woolf in 1941 of Terry's melodious voice, 'it was as if someone drew a bow over a ripe, richly seasoned 'cello; it grated, it glowed, and it growled . . . she filled the stage and all the other actors were put out, as electric lights are put out in the sun' (Woolf, *The Moment*, p. 165). But the quintessential quality which made her a great actor was comparable to Irving's own. Woolf goes on to define it:

now and again Nature creates a new part, an original part. The actors who act that part always defy our attempts to name them . . . when they come on the stage falls like a pack of cards and the limelights are extinguished. That was Ellen Terry's fate – to act a new part. And thus while other actors are remembered because they were Hamlet, Phèdre, or Cleopatra, Ellen Terry is remembered because she was Ellen Terry.   (Woolf, *The Moment*, p. 170)

With this combination of talent leading the cast, Irving could innovate. His Malvolio challenged popular preconceptions of the role, and anyone going to the Lyceum to see an ass being lampooned was going to be sorely disappointed. The reviewer for *Punch* commented:

Malvolio is no longer the middle-aged, conceited, puritanical donkey who is a fair butt for the malicious waiting-maid, two stupid sots, and a professional fool, but he becomes at once a grave and reverend signior, a Grand Duchess's trusted major-domo, faithfully discharging the duties of which he has an exaggerated opinion, and the very last person to be the subject of an idiotic practical joke, the stupidity of which is intensified by its wanton cruelty. And in the end he gains the public sympathy for his suffering, just as Shylock does.   (quoted in Pemberton, *Ellen Terry*, p. 254)

By playing the part in this way, Irving helped to develop the collective dramatic and critical responses to *Twelfth Night*. A cruel jest became a jest turned much too cruel, an interpretation which refreshed the understanding of Malvolio's character. It also looked back to Charles Lamb's reminiscences of Robert Bensley's 1792 portrayal (see Chapter 5), which several of Irving's reviewers commented on.

The setting was the Venetian Renaissance, which allowed for Elizabethan-style costume and Palladian architecture painted onto the backcloths. Viola and Sebastian, though, were in Balkan costume. Irving believed in mixing his metaphorical representations as it best suited the mood of the scene and characters. As Alan Hughes summarizes:

A separate visual metaphor was provided for each of his incongruous groups of characters, but each metaphor was naturalistically expressed in terms of time and place. Thus Toby and his crew held their midnight revel in an obviously English servants' hall where a fire blazed to keep the winter's chill at bay; but Olivia inhabited the sunny terrace and formal garden of an Italian villa, Orsino languished in the marble bosom of his Renaissance palace. . . . Only lighting was freed from the naturalistic convention, to show that Illyria was the realm of the imagination and not a Cook's tour.   (Hughes, *Henry Irving*, pp. 192–3)

Table 3 shows how Irving amalgamated and re-arranged the scenes.

Irving's portrayal was helped by his significant abridgement and rearrangement of the text (made available as a souvenir edition of the performance), from which 537 lines were cut (the equivalent to approximately half an hour), all of which brought Malvolio's tragic story to greater prominence. The production began darkly, with

Table 3   Henry Irving's arrangement of scenes

Oxford Shakespeare	Irving	Scenic setting
I.ii	I.i	Sea coast
I.iii	I.ii	Olivia's court-yard
I.iv and I.i	I.iii	Orsino's palace
I.v	II.i	Olivia's terrace
II.ii	II.ii	Road nearby
II.iii	II.iii	Olivia's servants' hall
II.iv	III.i	Orsino's palace
II.i	III.ii	Different part of the coast
II.v and III.i	III.iii	Olivia's garden
III.iii	IV.i	The market place
III.ii	IV.ii	Olivia's court-yard
III.iva until line 263	IV.iii	Olivia's garden
III.ivb and IV.i	IV.iv	The orchard end
IV.ii	IV.v	The dark room
IV.iii and V.i	V.i	Before Olivia's house

(Adapted from Alan Hughes, *Henry Irving, Shakespearean*, p. 254)

Viola's arrival in Illyria. Ellen Terry appeared silhouetted on a high rock, looking out over a moonlit ocean, rather like a painting by the great German Romantic painter Caspar David Friedrich. 'Her stately figure may be that of an abandoned Ariadne or an expectant Calypso; no one would ever suspect her to represent Viola' (William Archer, *Macmillan's Magazine*, August 1884; quoted in *Shakespearean Criticism*, 26, p. 205). When the production travelled to America, the *New York Times* commented on Terry's 'plaintive wail' as she asked 'And what should I do in Illyria? / My brother he is in Elysium' (I.ii.3–4; *New York Times*, 19 November 1884; quoted in *Shakespearean Criticism*, 26, p. 206). The romance of Orsino's (Mr Terriss) opening was amalgamated with Act I, scene iv (moonlit, not dark, and quasi-magical). The delay of any suggestion of lyricism was also reflected in the cutting of both 'O mistress mine' and 'Come away death'.

Sebastian (Mr F. Terry) and Antonio (Mr. H. Howe) did not appear until as late as Act III, scene ii, and their second scene together (Act III, scene iii in Shakespeare's text) was moved to appear just two scenes later and cut until Antonio's 'Hold, sir, here's my purse.' Sebastian's soliloquy at the beginning of Act IV, scene iii was cut entirely. Irving clearly wanted to delay the audience's knowledge and enjoyment of the inevitable comic outcome. Other cuts included Viola's soliloquy 'This fellow is wise enough to play the fool' (III.i.59–67) and internal abridgements to Malvolio's role and references to him, the cumulative effect of which removed the suggestion that Malvolio was merely a victim of circumstance, thereby heightening a sense of tragedy (for example: II.v.140–3, 'Be opposite . . . for thee'; III.ii.64–7, 'Yon gull . . . grossness'; III.iv.79–80, 'Well, Jove . . . thanked'; IV.ii.31–4, 'They have laid . . . courtesy'; 37–42, 'Why, it hath . . . dark'; 67–71, 'I would we were . . . upshot'; 74–80, 'Fool! . . . Who calls, ha?').

It was a Malvolio for the discerning theatre-goer in its clear delineation of the comic and tragic elements. Sir Edward Russell provided the following balanced and detailed account:

> Lean, lank, with self-occupied visage, and formal, peaked Spanish beard; dressed in close garb of black striped with yellow, and holding the steward's wand, in the lightness of which is something of fantastic symbolism, [Irving's Malvolio] steps on the stage with nose in air and eyes half shut, as if with singular and moody contemplation. He is visibly possessed of pride, of manners, and of intelligence. His pride, though intense, is not diseased, until the poison-dish of imagined love has been presented to him and has begun its work. Irving's gait; his abstraction of gaze, qualified by a polite observance of his lady, and a suspicious vigilance over his fellows in her service and her turbulent relations and followers; his sublime encounter with the Fool; his sententious observations on everything in general, and the infinite gravity yet imaginative airiness of his movements, carry the Malvolio of Shakespeare to a higher point of effect, probably, than it has ever reached on the stage.   (*Fortnightly*, 1 September 1884; quoted in Furness, *Variorum*, p. 400)

Writing with long hindsight, the actor Sir Frank Benson (*We Saw Him Act: A Symposium on the Art of Henry Irving*, ed. by H. A. Saintsbury and Cecil Palmer, 1939, quoted in *Shakespearean Criticism*, 26, pp. 207–10) thought that Irving's strong personality overcomplicated the role with psychological depth.

Other suggestions about how Irving spoke and acted the role of Malvolio can be gleaned from his working copy of the text, which, though sparsely annotated, contains underlinings which suggest emphasis. Irving shrugged on 'I marvel your ladyship takes delight in such a barren rascal' (I.v.78–9), and, 'formally approaching [Olivia] before speaking and then bowing', delivered his announcement of Cesario's arrival 'hastily surprised' (I.v.133–9). Underlining includes: II.ii.7–9, 'She adds . . . him'; II.iii.81, 'My masters, are you mad? Or what are you?' (Archer recorded in *Macmillan's Magazine* that Irving appeared in a 'marvellously spectral nightdress'; quoted in *Shakespearean Criticism*, 26, p. 205); II.v.110, 'I may command' (he looked up); and IV.ii.47 'as dark as hell'. It seems he started to make his entrance in the letter scene from Maria's 'Malvolio's coming down this walk' (II.v.13–14). He was smelling a flower, which he threw away on 'yeoman of the wardrobe' (II.v.37). Irving was still while reading the letter, and acted with his eyes. His eyes were shut during II.v.44–6: 'Calling . . . sleeping', and he changed to speak quickly for lines 49–52. He kissed the letter on 'Jove, I thank thee' (II.v.167). When he was rehearsing his smiles, his eyes were 'shut with rapture'. Curiously, the exchange with Olivia about going to bed (III.iv.27–9) appears to have been cut (either out of propriety, or because it was deemed too hilarious), but was re-instated. William Archer found that Irving's Malvolio created too much of an imbalance, and that any echoes of Shylock, as Irving exited at the end as a broken man, were merely melodramatic and gravely misplaced. Irving softened his final exit in light of this criticism. He appeared stronger and more dignified during Sir Topaz's interrogation and made sure that the scene was seriously comic, rather than tragic. He lightened his hair and complexion in order to modify the mood.

For all of Irving's serious overtones, Terry was her irrepressibly ebullient self. She was, however, in great pain during the opening night due to a poisoned thumb, which Bram Stoker's (Irving's manager) doctor brother had to lance between scenes. She wanted Viola to be very young (Terry herself was thirty-seven). The Balkan costume (cream and gold embroidered knee-length skirt with a blue

cap) accentuated her femininity, and steered away from any suggestion of a pantomime principal boy. Her sister Kate had doubled the
roles of Viola and Sebastian (not an unusual practice at the time).
Ellen played opposite her brother Fred Terry, who, she recollected,
managed to look like 'a *man* all over' (Terry, *Story*, p. 233), despite the
costume. Clement Scott thought that her Viola was:

> set in a most enchanting key. It is tender, human, graceful, consistently
> picturesque, and with humour as light as feather down. It will be reck-
> oned amongst the very best performances of this clever lady, and it grows
> upon the spectators as the play proceeds.   (quoted in Hiatt, *Ellen Terry*,
> pp. 177–8)

Scott goes on to add that her delivery of 'Excellently done, if God did
all' (I.v.256) was 'the very conceit of graceful impudence'. In the duel
she showed 'boyish petulance and obvious terror at the sight of the
sword blade' (Hiatt, *Ellen Terry*, p. 178). Since 'Sir Andrew was the
bigger coward, she fetched him a thwack across the bottom with the
flat of her sword' (Hughes, *Henry Irving*, p. 197). Yet she combined this
with a depiction of abject melancholy in her speech about 'patience
on a monument' (II.iv.110–18), 'passing behind [Orsino's] couch, she
dashed away a tear and looked down at him sorrowfully' (Hughes,
Henry Irving, p. 197). Terry, too, responded to criticism and changed
her performance in the light of it. The *Saturday Review* (12 July 1874)
noticed that she delivered the line 'I am the man' (II.ii.25) 'with an air
of pretty and intense amusement, and follows them by a charming
and laughing assumption of a mannish walk' (Hiatt, *Ellen Terry*,
p. 182). A week later, the same newspaper appreciated that Terry now
made sure that the following line, 'Poor lady, she were better love a
dream' (II.v.26), was tinged with a much greater pathos, to compen-
sate for any broadly comic gesture, or laughter she had provoked.
Ellen played the role for a total of sixteen out of thirty-nine performances (her sister Marion filled in for those she missed at the
Lyceum).

  Such were the achievements of Irving and Terry. Critical opinion
makes it clear that the Orsino, the senile Sir Toby (Mr D. Fisher), Sir
Andrew (Mr Wyatt) and the old Feste (Mr S. Calhaem) were miscast;

the comedians were unfunny. Olivia (Rose Leclercq) was noble and dignified, but past her youthful charms. The fact that she was only thirty-nine strengthens the sense of Terry's youthful portrayal.

Whether the audience or critics liked it or not, Irving's serious Malvolio was an innovation. As an actor he always tried to make his portrayal of a role fresh and creative. Echoes of Irving's interpretation and setting were still perceptible seventy-one years later in John Gielgud's 1955 production. Ellen Terry was Gielgud's great-aunt and she had seen Laurence Olivier (Gielgud's Malvolio) play Maria in a school production. Gielgud, too, suggested a Palladian Venetian setting; Olivier also had straw in his hair on his re-entrance towards the end. And, like Irving, he exited with a ferociously dark 'I'll be revenged on the whole pack of you,' at the end of a distinctly serious comedy.

Shakespeare Memorial Theatre, 1955

It had all the ingredients to be one of the most exciting opening nights in twentieth-century theatre history. A celebrated theatrical marriage (Sir Laurence Olivier and Vivien Leigh) was to lead what was heralded as the 96th Stratford Shakespeare season. Directed by Sir John Gielgud, the production created a storm of romantic antici- pation, 'with an actor knight in charge of the production and another actor knight and his lovely lady in the leads [as Malvolio and Viola]' (*Birmingham Mail*, 13 April 1955). It was to be the first time that Olivier and Gielgud had worked on stage together in twenty years (in 1935 they famously took it in turns to play the roles of Mercutio and Romeo), and the first time Olivier had acted in Stratford since 1922. In his film of *Richard III*, Olivier had directed Gielgud; now the roles were reversed. The announcement that Olivier and Leigh would also star as the Macbeths and as Lavinia and Titus Andronicus broke box office records: 600,000 applications for a total of just 80,000 seats in the 33-week run made it almost impossible to get a ticket. The box office received 400 telephone calls an hour, and people slept in the street all night to be sure of getting one of the 120 day-of-perfor- mance seats. It was also the first production of *Twelfth Night* to be staged in Stratford for eight years.

But there was something lacking. The reticence of the national papers after press-night (although delayed by the three-week newspaper strike) could not be concealed. Star-struck as they had entered the theatre, the critics almost uniformly stared into the cold light of day to deliver their lukewarm notices. The reviews combine highly measured appreciation with disappointment. The production was distinguished, over-charming and beautiful; although the text had been illuminatingly and poetically handled, there was a tendency for the cast to 'gabble', and since much of the action took place up-stage, audibility became a problem. The Shakespeare Memorial Theatre's proscenium arch was blamed for these poor effects. There was a great attention to detail, but the comedy was of a critical (even serious) kind which provoked neither present mirth nor present laughter. In short, the production's champagne lacked fizz; its stars lacked sparkle. Critics and audiences found it unfunny and unmoving; they also found it lacking in sentiment and warmth. It was up to the *Leamington Spa Courier* generously to sum up where the priorities of the production lay:

> John Gielgud's production was always pointed and alive, without ever attempting to startle; the care that was taken to see that the famous opening speech made sense in musical terms as well as conveying atmosphere and character was typical of its illumination of commonly unconsidered detail.   (15 April 1955)

Gielgud's *mise-en-scène* sought to combine linguistic with visual and emotional resonance. But it seems as though the attempt did not quite succeed well enough in its own terms, and that hopes for a legendary Illyria were wrecked in the tide of expectation. Kenneth Tynan, in a review which initially caused a rift between Olivier and himself (which later developed into a potent and famous actor–critic partnership), thought that the production:

> trod softly but sternly on the dream that Shakespearian comedy was a world of gaiety and refreshment. An astringent frost nipped the play, leaving bleakness behind it and an impression for which the polite word would be 'formal' and the exact word 'mechanical'.   (*Sunday Observer*, 24 April 1955)

The less imaginatively inclined *Daily Express* simply called it 'dull' (21 April 1955).

Gielgud himself knew he had missed the mark. Twenty-four years later he recalled:

> Somehow the production did not work, I do not know why. *Twelfth Night* must be one of the most difficult plays to direct, though it is one of my favourites. I have seen so many bad productions and never a perfect one. I would have given anything to have seen Granville-Barker's. . . . I acted Malvolio once at Sadler's Wells with Ralph Richardson as Sir Toby and enjoyed it, though that production was not very good either. It is so difficult to combine the romance of the play with the cruelty of the jokes against Malvolio, jokes which are in any case archaic and difficult. The different elements in the play are hard to balance properly. At Stratford I know that the actors were not very happy with the scenery, which was too far up-stage.   (Gielgud, *An Actor in His Time*, p. 176)

The rehearsals certainly drew out a clash in working practice between Gielgud and Olivier. Nine days before opening night, Gielgud confessed:

> Olivier is brilliant as Malvolio, though he is very ultra-realistic in his approach, and his gift of mimicry (as opposed to creative acting) sticks in my gizzard at times. His execution is so certain and skilled that it is difficult to convince him that he *can* be wrong in his own exuberance and should occasionally curb and check it in the interests of the general line and pattern of the play. The truth is he is a born autocrat, and must always be right. He has little respect for the critical sensitivity of others; on the other hand he is quite brilliant in his criticism of my directing methods and impatient with my hesitance and (I believe) necessary flexibility. He wants everything cut and dried at once, so that he may perfect [it?] with utter certainty of endless rehearsal and repetition – but he is good for me all the same, and perhaps I may still make a good thing of that divine play. (Letter to Stark Young, 3 April 1955, *Gielgud's Letters*, p. 180)

For all of its shortcomings, it is difficult not to fall a little in love with this production, or at least to be in love with Gielgud's idea of it, especially through the sensitively evocative photographic lens of Angus McBean. The style and spaciousness of the staging, its crisp and clearly delineated shapes of the Elizabethan costumes, palatial gardens and skylines all resonate in McBean's finely textured black and white. In 1901, three years before Gielgud was born, the critic and cartoonist Max Beerbohm, in reviewing Herbert Beerbohm Tree's *Twelfth Night*, had above all called for beauty:

> I maintain that Shakespeare's masterpieces are not at all degraded by a setting of beauty, that they deserve such setting, and by it are made more beautiful, and that anyone who by it is distracted from their own intrinsic beauty betrays in himself a lack of visual sense. (Wells, *Critical Essays*, p. 67)

Beerbohm's aesthetic was amply borne out by Gielgud's production.

The then 25-year-old Malcolm Pride designed the set and costumes. They were luxurious without being fussy, impressively grand without being intrusive. T. C. Worsley rejoiced 'to see Sir John breaking the fetish of the permanent set' (*New Statesman*, 23 April 1955). In fact there were at least seven major set changes (two intervals came down, at the end of II.iii and III.iii). Orsino's festooned, golden-lit Persian palace (including five on-stage musicians, two spear carriers, a servant fanning Orsino on his throne, who was also flanked by two courtiers) looked out onto an expansive seascape (the boat depicted sailing on it in the distance was very likely the one about to be shipwrecked). Orsino's other rooms were more enclosed, more heavily draped, and withdrawn (ideal for the private moments in I.iv and II.iv). Viola came ashore in what Pride described on the original costume design as 'a torn and water stained thin silk dress, with broken pearl ornaments' (reproduced in the 1955 souvenir programme). With 'a few stray sapphires and pearls in [her] hair' she was like a fairy-tale princess from the ocean. There was something almost siren-like about her initial appearance. A gauze depicted waves rolling onto a beach, crashing against rocks, with the shipwrecked boat in the distance. Act II, scene v, gave a visual impression of ornamentation and secrecy at the back of Olivia's Palladian house, styled with lofty, curled wrought iron gates and topiary hedges: a maximum amount of cosmetic order at precisely the moment when Malvolio is being deceived. In another part of the same garden (for the last third of the production) two immense epic hedges jutted squarely in from both sides. Malvolio's cross-gartered left leg appeared from behind the hedge on stage right in Act III, scene iv, followed by the peering of his inane smiles of glee.

Michael Billington, writing in 1987, gave a thumbnail sketch of Olivier's greatness as an actor:

> a formidable interpretative intelligence that intuitively searches for new meanings in the great classic roles; an incisive voice that has the directional force and cutting edge of a laser; eyes that can communicate powerful emotion over a large distance . . . a mimetic relish that may spring, if we are to believe *Confessions of an Actor* [Olivier's autobiography], from self-doubt and even self-disgust; a boundless energy that has meant, over the years, that each new Olivier performance was as much a creative event as, say, a new novel by Graham Greene or a new film by Orson Welles.   (O'Connor, *Olivier in Celebration*, p. 72)

Eye and nose make-up were always important to Olivier: Malvolio's thick black brows were used to cast scornful glances over an accentuated beak-like nose. He was a servant who knew his place, a thoroughly unlikable man, with a supercilious, turkeycock walk (II.v.28), fussy, but not absurd, with a tall, Puritan hat, who 'looked as if he lived on a diet of sour green apples' (*Nottingham Guardian*, 13 April 1955), but ever-sensitive to facial nuance and bodily gesture. For most critics, Olivier took the role too seriously, 'more sinned against than sinning' (*Wolverhampton Express and Star*, 13 April 1955, invoking *The Tragedy of King Lear*, III.iv.59–60), which meant that there was not sufficient contrast between the low comic scenes and the high romance. One returns to Gielgud's own sense of lament before opening night: Olivier was making sure he did everything his own way, even if this led to a generic imbalance. J. C. Trewin commended the fresh approach that Olivier brought to the role:

> I have seen Malvolios by the score. Some have been more immediately comic. None has been developed more logically and with less apparent effort. . . . He is, very simply, Malvolio: he takes us back to the man's past, and makes us speculate about his future.   (*Illustrated London News*, 23 April 1955)

Tynan crisply added to the critical debate the following day by saying Olivier's 'sun peeped through the chintz curtains of the production ... a self-made snob, aspiring to consonance with the quality but ever betrayed by the vowel sounds from Golders Green' (*Sunday Observer*, 24 April 1955). Gielgud was later to recall:

> Olivier was set on playing Malvolio in his own particular rather extravagant way. He was extremely moving at the end, but he played the earlier scenes like a Jewish hairdresser, with a lisp and an extraordinary accent. (Gielgud, *An Actor in His Time*, p. 178)

Ivor Brown thought he sounded foreign, 'with the r's softened into w's ("Some have gweatness thwust upon them [sic., II.v.136–7]")' (quoted in Cottrell, *Laurence Olivier*, p. 258), and he struggled over the pronunciation of 'slough' (II.v.139), which helplessly betrayed his working-class origins.

In Act I, scene v, he stood behind Feste (Edward Atienza), who curled up at Olivia's (Maxine Audley) feet, for nurture and protection from Malvolio's withering looks. He looked amazed when Olivia told him to run after Cesario, and offered the ring from the end of his staff of office, as though trying to avoid infection (II.ii). Feste sang 'O mistress mine' sitting at a table-top harpsichord (the musical settings were by Leslie Bridgewater; both they and the singing were much commended). During the great drinking scene, Feste mocked Malvolio's staff by brandishing the poker for 'Peg-o'-Ramsey' (II.iii.72). Malvolio's entrance was heralded by Maria's (Angela Baddeley) serious attempts to quieten the three revellers. She blew out the candles on 'for the love o' God, peace', and Feste crouched under the table just before Malvolio came onto the stage. He appeared in a nightgown and nightcap, carrying a candle holder. Malvolio removed the table cloth before he spoke and let it drop; Maria began to tidy up the cups a few lines later, on Malvolio's 'Sir, Toby, I must be round with you' (II.iii.89). Sir Toby (Alan Webb, who stepped in to replace the recently injured Brewster Mason) was like a gentlemanly retired colonel. He took up the poker and brandished it threateningly at Malvolio on 'Shall I bid him go?' (II.iii.102), while Michael Denison's clottish and fantastical Sir Andrew barred the only exit. Sir Toby lifted Malvolio's chain of office with the poker on 'Go, sir, rub your chain with crumbs' (II.iii.111–12). The end of the scene and of the first part of the play seems to have worked beautifully as a contrasting moment of relaxation. Maria was yawning; Sir Andrew yawned as he said 'I was adored once, too' (II.iii.169). The blackjack of drink was empty: a prompt for Sir Toby to ask his companion to send for more money (II.iii.170–1), before returning the poker to the fire. The clock struck half-past one as Sir Toby said 'Come, come' (II.iii.178). The revels temporarily ended; Feste snored, Sir Andrew hiccoughed, and the poker hissed.

While Malvolio was reading the letter he walked in a big circle around the great garden followed by the three eavesdroppers. He kissed the letter on 'if thou entertain'st my love' (II.v.164). At the end of the speech before his exit he fell off the seat with excitement – 'I begged him not to do it' (Gielgud, *An Actor in His Time*, p. 178) – laughed at himself and took out a pocket mirror to register his smile. The tables were turned nicely in terms of the stage picture for the Sir Topaz scene. Feste (who had hidden under the table in Act II, scene iii) looked menacingly down onto Malvolio, who peered up with great self-control from the trap-door (he conveniently ducked down out of sight while Feste was pretending to talk to Sir Topaz). Ever the rationalist Olivier's Malvolio offered Feste his ring on 'it shall advantage thee more than ever the bearing of the letter did' (IV.ii.112–13). Feste pushed Malvolio's head down with his foot on his reiterating this ('I'll requite it in the highest degree', IV.ii.119), and shut the prison's trap-door.

Although Gielgud found Leigh's Viola enchanting, whilst admitting she was not a born actress (Gielgud, *Letters*, p. 180), the critics, on the whole, found her monotone ('dazzlingly' so, as far as Tynan was concerned, 'like steady rain on corrugated tin roofing', *Sunday Observer*, 24 April 1955). She used a lower voice register for Cesario, and her costume (twinning Trader Faulkner's Sebastian with cropped, boyish wigs) had something of the pantomime's principal boy about it. She stared ardently into the audience with sadness during Act II, scene iv: 'patience on a monument' captured beautifully in the stage image of Orsino (Keith Michell, who attracted unanimously poor notices) sitting raised on a small fur-covered platform, while Cesario curled up adoringly at his feet. She was still and intense; it was a controlled and dignified, rather than a bewildered, portrayal. With Olivia she was more satirical, turning away from being touched on the shoulder, on 'You might do much' (I.v.266). For III.i.143–54 Olivia curled up helplessly on the floor, with her arms around Cesario's legs, imploring him to love her. She spoke slowly. The impassively pitying Cesario slowly helped her up during the speech which followed. The emphasis was on stillness and on clear quietness.

In the closing moments, Malvolio re-entered from the trap-door, wisps of straw in his hair, a broken, unloving and unlovable man. Feste plucked his lute strings as Time's whirligig brought 'in its revenges' (V.i.367) and Malvolio's shattering cry 'I'll be revenged on the whole pack of you' arose from an extremely deep wound.

Leigh changed into a beautiful and grand wedding dress, as Duchess Viola of Illyria, for the bows (her 'woman's weeds', V.i.267); Olivier made an apparently humble curtain-call speech at the end of the first night. As for Gielgud, he was already preparing Benedick and Lear opposite Peggy Ashcroft's Beatrice and Cordelia. He slipped away to Venice for ten days immediately after the opening night: not *quite* far enough away from Il*larry*ira.

Royal Shakespeare Company, 1974

Peter Gill's exploration of sexuality gave his production an overridingly serious edge. He was clearly interested in the darker side of comedy. 'The erotic undertones of the play would have been audible from the opposite bank of the Avon' (Speaight, *Quarterly*, 25, p. 392) and 'it was generally agreed' that Gill's production 'worked much better for the serious characters than for the comic ones' (Potter, *Text and Performance*, p. 68). Coming only two years after the end of John Barton's already legendary, melancholic and autumnal *Twelfth Night* (see Chapter 5), the newly arrived Gill made a fresh departure. His own homosexuality encouraged him to present an unabashed and at times highly charged production, 'reaching for the audience's bisexuality' (Thomson, *Survey*, p. 145).

The uncompromisingly spacious setting (basically an adaptation of the same boxed stage which was also used for *King John*, *Cymbeline* and *Richard II*) meant that the production relied strongly on the actors' bodies and vocal range to dress the stage, to create the atmosphere and tell the story. The effect concentrated attention on the language and the relationships between the characters. Gill did not want to impose too much conceptually, and pared down visual distractions to enable clarity of expression and to let the audience in. The overall rhythmic impression was of 'long entrances and exits', of 'choreographed movement on a bare stage' (Thomson, *Survey*, p. 144). The designer, William Dudley, coloured the walls to give the impression of sky blending into sand: pale blue, pinks, peaches and a tawny gold. A central track allowed for the efficient setting of furniture from adroitly manoeuvred side panels: an impressionistic but self-contained, rustically half-timbered room for the drinking scene in II.iii., a tea-table for Olivia in III.iv, and three green-leaved trees. These first appeared for Act I, scene iii, suggesting the orchard, and conveyed the impression that much of the action for Olivia's household took place out of doors. It was springtime in Gill's Illyria.

But there was one overarching visual imposition peering down onto the proceedings. An erotic, pale mural of Narcissus gazing languorously into a pool adorned the central panel, which moved forward 'to create the two up stage entrances very much in the position of Elizabethan doors' (Thomson, *Survey*, p. 144). Critics were divided over the appropriateness of the Narcissus image. J. W. Lambert made the obvious connection with Malvolio being 'sick of self love' (I.v.85), but also, in Gill's production, Feste (Ron Pember). Neither can 'smash the mirror [nor] at last look outward lovingly to other people' (*Sunday Times*, 25 August 1974). Frank Marcus was less certain:

> if everybody's action were prompted by self-love, the question of choice would not arise. There would be no conflict, no mistaken identities, and no play. A case of narcissism might be made against the bi-sexual Duke because the object of his passion, Olivia (Mary Rutherford), is a pert, frisky little thing who could not be described as mysteriously beautiful. But it is not a watertight concept for any of the others.   (*Sunday Telegraph*, 25 August 1974)

For Victoria Radin (*Observer*, 25 August 1974), this aspect of the design was reminiscent of Oscar Wilde's *The Picture of Dorian Grey*. Both Lambert and Marcus attempt to read the image literally, seeking parallels among the characters, whereas Radin allows for a wider interpretation which reflects on Gill's wider interest in the sexual atmosphere. Only B. A. Young (*Financial Times*, 23 August 1974) mentions the inclusion in the theatre programme of a quotation from R. D. Laing:

Narcissus fell in love with his image, taking it to be another . . .

Jill is a distorting mirror to herself.
Jill has to distort herself to appear undistorted to herself.

To undistort herself, she finds Jack to distort her distorted image in his distorting mirror.
She hopes that his distortion of her distortion may undistort her image without her having to distort herself.

The image, it seems, was also there to keep ever-present the idea of *Twelfth Night* exploring lost as well as refracted selves (through imagination, mourning, drunkenness, disguise, and, most powerfully, shipwreck). One of Shakespeare's challenges for his characters and audience is to ask how far we might be willing to change and become vulnerable and open to the love of others; Gill's symbolic illustration might have suggested that to follow the example of Narcissus could lead to an irrevocable and tragic metamorphosis, as in Ovid's tale, and that we need to take a few risks in love: 'in delay there lies no plenty' (II.iii.48).

The explicitly literary context of Gill's production also included two quotations from Shakespeare's Sonnets (numbers 20, 2, 33, and 144 were printed in the programme), which were faintly written on the walls of the set: 'O learn to read what silent love hath writ' (Sonnet 23) and 'O know, sweet love, I always write of you' (Sonnet 76). The original context for these lines concerns the inability of language fully to express love's feelings. In Sonnet 23, there is also the suggestion of a love repressed, just as homosexual desire may, in the world of *Twelfth Night*, 'for fear of trust' (Sonnet 23, line 5), face anxieties about its self-expression. The two quotations which Gill used to frame his production would also have prompted self-reflection on the part of the audience in their puzzlement to work out why the words were there. The image of Narcissus, then, might have worked as a point of convergence for many different questions of self-hood and sexuality: as much a touchstone for the audience, as for the characters and actors on stage.

The sensuously positioned, almost naked Narcissus might have also prompted a degree of mental undressing in the imagined world of the characters, as well as, possibly, in the real world of the audience. The costumes, designed by Deirdre Clancy, were resolutely and exquisitely Elizabethan: rich silks and velvets, ruffs and handmade suede shoes, corduroys and taffetas. The famous Elizabethan painter and portrait miniaturist Nicholas Hilliard was mentioned by J. W. Lambert in relation to the overall visual impact (*Sunday Times*, 25 August 1974). The costumes, coupled with the overall design, meant that the production had visual similarities with Gill's 2004 Royal Shakespeare Company (RSC) *Romeo and Juliet*. Olivia, Maria and two other ladies-in-waiting (there were plenty of servants to help to people the space) all appeared in black for Act I, scene v. By the time they re-entered in Act III, scene i, Olivia was wearing a brightly coloured orange silk dress, Maria (Patricia Hayes) was wearing tomato-coloured cotton, and the two attendants were dressed in sage green and gold: such was the transformative power of Viola's (Jane Lapotaire) first visit. Viola herself appeared in a full-skirted rose-coloured (cf. 'For women are as roses', II.iv.37) gown after the shipwreck in Act I, scene ii, sea-stained and damp, with long, straggling, wet hair (which she began to pin up, on 'I'll serve this Duke', I.ii.52). On her next appearance, in Act I, scene iv, boyishly shadow-boxing with Valentine, she appeared androgynous, with cropped hair, wearing a crisp doublet and hose in the white and cream satin purity of Orsino's (John Price) servant livery. Orsino himself wore a white linen doublet trimmed with gold, and cream tights.

Sir Toby (David Waller) and Sir Andrew (Frank Thornton) were well dressed in brown and muted-coloured linens and corduroys, the latter with a prominently positioned white leather purse attached to his waist, always ready to part with money. Malvolio's (Nicol Williamson) black velvet costume:

> was striped with white lines of various thickness and density and topped with a ruff. It had a *trompe l'oeil* effect, seeming to hold a tiny head an impossible distance from the bottom of the long, mean legs. (Thomson, *Survey*, p. 145)

Williamson may have had problems keeping on his cross-garters. The archival photographs taken at the technical rehearsal include rare images of a Malvolio tying up his own gartering. In Act II, scene iii he sported an elaborately flowing dressing gown, carefully embroidered around the base in multi-colours. This quasi-motley was to become painfully true for him. Feste was poorly and rustically dressed in unhemmed, faded motley. He was clearly outside the economic basis which supported the folly of those around him. In Act II, scene iv he wore a baggy, loosely crocheted cardigan. The little drum he carried evoked visual echoes of Richard Tarlton, the famous Elizabethan comic.

Pember's overall portrayal, though, was more bitter than funny. Several reviewers noticed his Cockney accent. Fabian (Brian Hall) also had a Cockney accent, but the production did not pursue any thematic, or potential, interpretative connections between these two roles. Lois Potter recalls that Pember's Feste 'made some spectators uncomfortable' (Potter, *Text and Performance*, p. 63). Benedict Nightingale in the *New Statesman* (14 February 1975, on the show's transfer to London) reported that Feste:

> mutters at Olivia, growls at Viola, rages at Orsino, sneers at Malvolio, and then turns on the audience with such savagery that the closing line 'we'll strive to please you every day', comes across as a promise to flay us *en masse* in the foyer.

Pember's Feste was trenchantly proud of his social position, closer to Thersites in *Troilus and Cressida* or Apemantus in *Timon of Athens* (*Sunday Times*, 25 August 1974). Pember's portrayal made it believable that this Feste slept rough, that it mattered where his next meal was

coming from, and, in the words of Jane Lapotaire in a private interview, 'he made you understand all court jesters, what they were
about, how they lived'. After the interpolated jig, which Feste
performed with other cast members at the beginning of the second
half, he gave Viola short shrift for her daring to assume he was a
beggar (III.i.8–11). For Thomson, Pember's portrayal was 'malevo-
lently saturnine' and he recalls a comparison made with Bosola in *The
Duchess of Malfi* (Thomson, *Survey*, p. 146). Malvolio's prison consisted
of him sitting on a low stool with his hands tied and the rope chained
to the floor, in a pool of dim light (similar staging was used in Bill
Alexander's 1987 RSC production, in which Antony Sher's Malvolio
was imprisoned against a pillory-like stake). Feste carried a lantern
with him during his visit, eerily lighting up the darkness and heightening the effect of intimidation for the audience. But Pember was
genuinely amusing as Sir Topaz, which made Malvolio's call for
revenge all the more uncomfortable. Feste's final lines about
Malvolio were defiantly unsentimental.

Malvolio was possessed of all the wild and dangerous qualities
which Nicol Williamson was known for bringing with him onto the
stage. He had played Coriolanus the season before and was due to
play Macbeth for the RSC within two months of *Twelfth Night* having
opened. His tight-lipped authority was expressed with a slightly hesi-
tant and softly spoken voice which in the main only used his bottom
lip. It was a grotesque performance, with something of the simmer-
ing Scottish pastor about it, replete with a proud, crane-like walk.
The smile he managed to force at II.v.167, 'like a winter sun breaking
through the clouds' (Speaight, *Quarterly*, p. 392), was a key moment in
Williamson's painfully absurd performance. In the final scene, he left
the stage having torn the letter up with a shattering and agonized cry.
Speaight mentions an excessive 'fourfold repetition' of Malvolio's
exit line (Speaight, *Quarterly*, p. 392); Lambert mentions him covering
his face and snarling, so perhaps Williamson experimented with its
delivery during the run. His aim, though, was to leave a nasty flavour
behind him with Malvolio's exit.

'The breeding was preserved with the belching' in David Waller's
Sir Toby (Speaight, *Quarterly*, p. 392), but he also suggested something
of a man wounded by grief for the death of a brother and a nephew.

He was cast old, as was Frank Thornton's 'exquisitely vapid' Sir Andrew (Speaight, *Quarterly*, p. 392), whose 'long face and longer silence […] preceded his lifeless question, "Shall we set about some revels?" ', I.iii.127 (Thomson, *Survey*, p. 145). Maria, too, was strongly cast. Patricia Hayes mainly brought her natural comedy and a sense of the maternal to the role; she slapped Feste for mentioning Sir Toby's feelings for her (I.v.26). She was an old Maria, which made sense in relation to the youth of Mary Rutherford's Olivia. Rutherford (who had played Hermia in Peter Brook's famous 1970 RSC *A Midsummer Night's Dream*) was quite tactile and provocative with Malvolio, which he mistook as sexual flirtation. With Viola, Rutherford's performance admitted an ambiguity as to whether she was enjoying touching a page, or someone she recognized primarily as feminine.

Robert Lloyd's Sebastian was praised for looking very similar to Viola (though stepped shoes had to be used in the final scene to make sure he was the same height as Lapotaire's Viola). His Antonio (Paul Moriarty) was definite in loyalty and love for his young master, but closed and private. He took him in his arms when Sebastian started to cry in Act II, scene i, and when Antonio thought himself betrayed he grasped Viola around the neck at III.iv.356, and pushed her hard away from him at the end of that speech. Homosocial rather than homosexual Antonio and Sebastian might have been (Frank Marcus is evasive in his *Sunday Telegraph* review when he compares them to footballers hugging after a goal), but the overarching mood was definitely one in which the continuum of sexuality could be explored. Sebastian lavished innocent affection on Antonio, who responded diffidently: it was less easy to be gay in 1974.

John Price's Orsino was first discovered lounging on cushions (echoing the Narcissus behind him), flanked by Curio (Louis Sheldon) and his other attendants. Composer George Fenton was playing his own on-stage music on a solitary violin as a member of the court. The cushions, beautiful courtiers and violin playing returned for 'Come away death' in Act II, scene iv, but this time Orsino and Viola took centre stage, sitting on the floor. Orsino, bare chested, medallioned, and loosely clothed was clearly entranced. He had already fondled the front of her doublet in Act I, scene iv, on 'all is semblative a woman's part' (line 34). In Act II, scene iv, Viola tried to move away on 'A little, by your favour', and a little further on 'Of your complexion' (ll. 24–5). Orsino pulled Viola towards him on 'About your years', lifting her back into a kneeling position on 'Too old, by heaven' (II.iv.27–8). He held her by the left hand during the song, after which, once the stage had cleared, they moved closer still. His legs were open and Viola was sitting in a curled position between them, close enough for her left leg to be in complete contact with his left leg. He took hold of her head and turned it intimately towards him on 'But died thy sister of her love, my boy?' (II.iv.119). The moment of their togetherness trembled with a vulnerable beauty.

In an interview, Jane Lapotaire recalled how Gill used to give line readings to the cast (which many actors object to). She believes that this was encouraged by Gill's Welsh origins. He heard the music in the language, which he wanted conveyed.

> It took me ages to capture the right distinction between 'What *country* friends is this?' and 'What country friends is *this*?', which is as Peter wanted it. The first arises from a matter of fact, of geographical concern, the second implies an encounter with something magical and alien.

Similarly,

> John Price and I had a tendency to be lyrical. Peter thought we didn't have to do this with Shakespeare's language and he would make Orsino go for a short run before starting the play so that John had just the right kind of relaxation in his voice for that opening speech.

Lapotaire praised Shakespeare's stage-craft in making sure that Viola has just enough time to change from a full Elizabethan-style dress into a doublet and hose during Act I, scene iii. 'My disguise as a boy had a curious effect on the company. I would often be mauled play-fully in the wings by some of my male colleagues, for whom the disguise seemed to permit that kind of friendly expression.' Gill had a great eye for detail: 'I had a colourful scarf around my waist which had to be exactly the same length as that which Sebastian wore.' Lapotaire recalled the rare quality of 'macho gentleness' which Price brought to the role of Orsino, and how Gill thought about Act II, scene iv, being 'a double whammy for the gay guys in Shakespeare's audience', especially with a boy originally having played Viola. 'I felt cheated out of the songs which Viola doesn't get to sing. "Come away death" is so plangent, that it could be sung by Viola, whose own brother she believes has had no proper burial.' The production made the greatest emotional investment in the reunion of Viola and Sebastian.

> Sebastian was masked by Antonio in our staging to delay my seeing him. 'Most wonderful' brought the house down because of the miracle of the moment, as well as Olivia's sexual interests. The moment made both me and Sebastian cry. I remember us being surprised at how moving it was. Getting my beloved Orsino was fine only because I'd got my brother back first.

In the final moments, Antonio was initially included in the dance with Olivia, Sebastian, Viola and Orsino, but was then excluded. The group exited and Antonio was left on his own, bemused, desiring, aching, as Feste presented the final song to the audience.

Royal Shakespeare Company 2005

As a director of Shakespeare, Michael Boyd's successes have mainly been with the histories and the tragedies (*Henry VI Parts One, Two and Three*, and *Richard III* in 2000–1 and *Hamlet* in 2004). There was a stark and challenging *Romeo and Juliet* in 2000, a brooding and unsettling *The Tempest* in 2002. His *Troilus and Cressida* (1998) and *Measure for Measure* (1998–9) achieved polemical positions in their disruptions of generic tone and state politics. His *Much Ado About Nothing* (1996–7) complicated the comedy with its visual cleverness. And there was the spare, stylish, and controversially sexy *A Midsummer Night's Dream* in 1999. All of these productions avoided sentimentality and their comedy was absurd and dispassionate. What Michael Boyd's *Twelfth Night* shared with the rest of his output was a genuine attempt to look at a well-trodden play as though for the very first time. Combined with a directorial flair for political tragedies and histories, the result was predominantly dark in tone, a production rich in interpersonal relationships, but one which in the end did not touch all of the play's many hearts.

Waves breaking against the shore and the squawk of an occasional seagull could be heard as the audience arrived and settled into their seats. We were heading towards a shipwreck, were being reminded of the passing of time, the effect of experience on love, and approaching the gulling of Malvolio. The designer Tom Piper is fond of open, uncluttered spaces. His work with Peter Brook means that he is interested in an organic process of creative design, as the dramatic happening itself evolves. His Illyria was a bare, elegant, stylishly spacious wooden-walled stage, of a piece with his designs for Boyd's *A Midsummer Night's Dream* and *Hamlet*. The effect was typically disarming and set up a challenge for the actors to bring their own sense of a social reality onto stage with them.

The opening scene was set for a band. There were several music stands and an upright piano. The musicians entered and a curtain on the back wall rose to reveal a large, dominating pair of eyes painted on wooden slats. Actually, it was the upper third of a female face. The effect was alienating, unsettling, and conveyed a sense of Narcissistic self-regard, 'beauty truly blent', and 'two grey eyes, with lids to them' (I.v.228 and 236–7). The image was modelled on Olivia's (Aislín McGuckin) face. Her eyes were the literally realized object of Orsino's (Barnaby Kay) fantasy. A finely draped curtain provided the plain and austere backdrop for Olivia's palace until she unveiled herself to Viola (Kananu Kirimi) at I.v.223. After that point the eyes began to appear in Olivia's palace, too (they were present during the eavesdropping in II.v), a visual metaphor for youth, intensity and surveillance. The design's economy meant that a parted black curtain was lowered to create the box-tree.

The largely bare and open space was dressed partly by suspended objects which had either been part of the action or re-entered the action at intervals. The music stands were flown above the stage at the end of the first scene, as was the upright piano. They remained suspended as a visual memory of Orsino's court and held open the promise of further music. The piano descended on several occasions:

at the beginning of Act I, scene v (Feste hid behind it as Maria chased him with a black arm-band), the beginning of Act II, scene iv, and Act III, scene i. Viola, the Sea Captain and a sailor descended by ropes from the shipwreck at the beginning of Act I, scene ii. Sebastian and Antonio descended in a flying boat, nose-diving vertically straight downwards at the beginning of Act II, scene i. The boat, too, remained suspended above the front centre of the stage for the rest of the production, reminding us of their escape, and the confusion as well as salvation heralded by their entrance.

Orsino's decadence and excess was stressed by the large number of musicians who attended on him, by the evening-dressed singer who poured out her song in a varying, powerful wail, 'a dying fall' (I.i.4), as well as by an inflated sense of Orsino's own ego. After entering and sitting down, Orsino stared into the audience and took so long to start the famous opening line that a member of the band got the first laugh of the evening by opening his newspaper to read until receiving further notice from his Count and master. Unusually, Feste (Forbes Masson) was present, too, responding to 'that strain again' (I.i.4) as though it were a command, as he took up the wailing where the female singer left off. 'Enough, no more' saw Orsino jerk a glass of water into Feste's careworn face (pale, whitened skin, black heavy-ringed eyes and reddish ears). The splash of water jokily prefigured the shipwreck we were about to see. When Orsino finished his opening meditation about the bank of violets, the band gave him a round of applause after the words 'giving odour'. Orsino's 'Enough, no more' also became an order for them all to stop clapping (I.i.7).

The same band assembled again at the beginning of Act II, scene iv in their nightclothes, exhausted and cross. Orsino appeared bare-chested in burgundy silk pyjama bottoms and a matching full-skirted dressing-gown. A dehydrated Feste (still drunk from the revelling in Act II, scene iii) took an effervescent hangover cure before commencing 'Come away death'. This Orsino would have music at any time of day or night, and his courtiers had to obey his every selfish need. Kay's Orsino was full of seething sexuality, frustrated and bated, as his bear-like name suggests: 'a man who should have iced water poured over him', in the words of Benedict Nightingale (*The Times*, 30 April 2005). Orsino moved close to Cesario during the song because his sexual feelings were stronger than both of them, rather than out of any obvious homoerotic desire. He attempted, but failed, to kiss Cesario after 'and yet I know not' (II.iv.121). The band also followed him to Olivia's palace at the beginning of Act V, scene i. Orsino was wealthy, successful and could do nothing by halves; his exaggerated generosity spoke volumes about his own profound insecurities. The musicians were quietly dismissed before the stage became really full. In an interview, Kay said that Orsino is genuinely in love with the page but, when Cesario turned out to be Viola, it was 'like Christmas'.

A pervasive but not quite all-embracing sexual energy ran through the whole production. Feste was attracted to Maria (Meg Fraser), a fresh interpretation that did much to explain points of narrative direction as well as provide further strands of humour and pathos. There was a decidedly sexual thrill in their apparently harmless chase (instigated by Maria) at the beginning of Act I, scene v. In order to silence the drunken antics of Sir Toby (Nicky Henson on press night, Clive Wood further into the run), Sir Andrew (John Mackay) and Feste, Maria, who appeared in a négligé, walked to the front of the stage, turned her back on the audience, and flashed them during their brief burst of the carol 'The Twelve Days of Christmas' (II.iii.79–80). She stunned them into sudden and comic silence. When, a little later, Maria was sharing her plot against Malvolio with the midnight revellers, a stage picture brought her seated centrally between Sir Toby and Feste, downstage left. Feste tried hard to attract her attention and flirt with her, but she was clearly too captivated by Sir Toby's encouragement (Shakespeare gives Feste nothing to say in this scene from line 110). Feste picked up his suitcase of wine and left before the end of the scene. Maria had neglected him and her neglect helped obliquely to explain why he was absent from the eavesdropping scene in Act II, scene v. Michael Billington referred to Maria as a 'voluptuous tease' and to the 'memorably lovelorn Feste' (the *Guardian*, 30 April 2005). When Feste said to Viola, 'I do care for something' (III.i.27), it was loaded with the pangs of unrequited love. This Feste knew all about that from spending time with Orsino.

Sexual energy seemed sublimated in the extravagant, physical gestures of Sir Andrew, especially in his sudden fits of dancing, tosses of the head, lunges and crossed scorpion legs in the duel. A sexual frustration was also apparent in the way he occasionally expressed himself ('Je hope so', his comic reply to Viola's 'Et vous aussi, votre serviteur' in III.i.71–2). Malvolio (Richard Cordery) sublimated his sexual fantasies in repeated and showy displays of self-indulgent karate gestures as he entered the box-tree scene. He appeared to Olivia wearing a full black and yellow leather biker's suit, a sexy and provocative costume which it was amusing to think he had been hiding in his closet. Olivia entered and felt her own breasts in a private moment of sexual fantasy (III.iv.1–4). At her entrance in Act IV, scene i she brandished a bondage-style whip. She had finally come to take control of Cesario (now Sebastian) and cracked the whip with authority, catching the back of Sir Andrew's ankles as he hurried off stage. In contrast, Viola seemed curiously sexless. Although she exaggerated masculine gesture on occasion (we saw her 'adjust [her] willy', as the prompt book has it, at the beginning of Act I, scene iv), Kirimi was more interested in portraying naivety than vulnerability and sexual risk. There was no hint at all of a sexual relationship between Sebastian (Gurpreet Singh) and Antonio (Neil McKinven). Their bond seemed more to be one of duty.

For a production spare in its staging, there were several visual conceits. The painted eyes and box-tree have already been mentioned. The Sir Topaz scene started in darkness until Feste blew out his lantern. The stage was then fully lit, but we were led to believe that the characters were in pitch darkness. Malvolio entered with his legs and body apparently tied to an off-stage stake. He almost had enough rope to hang himself and was only just prevented from walking off the edge of the stage. Feste managed to place his left hand accidentally on Maria's left breast. She had kissed him warmly at the beginning of the scene but now left him, cold and in the dark. This gave a melancholy edge to his song 'Hey Robin', and especially the lines 'My lady is unkind, pardie' and 'She loves another'.

This was a production rich in relationships and striated with sexual desire. The suspended objects, like the narrative's effect on its characters, reminded us that love makes everything 'unstaid and skittish in all motions else' (II.iv.17). But love had been tricked out of this production, if not quite banished from it altogether. Apart from Feste (and his love for Maria was always somewhere *just* beyond the text), desire and passion remained objectified: a succession of hard-edged, sexual gestures. The production thus lost out on melancholy and comedy. Lyricism, too, which might have inspired and complicated unforced affection, was lost. The final moments (from the reunion of Viola and Sebastian) opened up the back wall of the set onto Olivia's garden, full of gaudy artificial flowers. There were more suspended music stands, encrusted with sheet music. Some of the pages of music dropped onto the flowers. It was a graveyard-like wonderland, as well as merely an outdoor setting. The couples paired up and exited upstage left. As Feste began his song, Maria and Sir Toby walked to cross upstage right, deserving each other and resolutely going their own ways together. A few more pages of sheet music dropped to the earth, blessing and nourishing the place beneath, like rain.

This survey of one hundred and twenty years of *Twelfth Night* has included four productions with a range of affinities and differences, from Irving's highly victimized Malvolio to a flying boat, from Terry's overtly feminine Viola to Lapotaire's boyish and vulnerable Cesario, from the visual grandeur of Gielgud's production to an empty wooden space. These productions have brought much to the service of this play in key stages of its theatrical life, and there will always be a great deal more to bring, as we reflect our own hopes and desires through the comic lens of Shakespeare's text.

4 The Play on Screen

Films are texts read linearly, like novels. They do not rely on the dimensions of space, as theatrical performances do, in order to make meaning. Whilst the interpretative processes which films inspire are ever changing, the filmic moment itself is fixed, like paint on a canvas: a point of empirical certainty against which to measure and evaluate different readings. Films are helpful because of the range of interpretative choices they make possible. Although the obvious difference of their artistic medium makes many of the effects achievable by a camera lens impossible to achieve in a stage production (and vice-versa), three contrasting versions of *Twelfth Night* filmed over fifteen years (between 1988 and 2003) offer a range of dramatic and visual interpretation, worthy of consideration. The fixity of film means that the interpretation remains locked in time, but this in itself can bring all the rewards of an old master or a manuscript. The three versions of *Twelfth Night* depict distinctly different Illyrian worlds and moods, offer contrasting perspectives on characterization and relationships, and allow the viewer to appreciate how the play text has been (and may be) abridged and adapted. They also hold within themselves the potential for Shakespeare's language at best to sound freshly minted to successive audiences, at worst to seem stale or old-fashioned: much can be learned from the best and worst of times.

Kenneth Branagh's production for his Renaissance Theatre Company was filmed for Thames Television in 1988. The point of departure is Viola's (Frances Barber) 'What country, friends, is this?' (I.ii.1: transposition of the first two scenes has not been uncommon on the stage), spoken in a neutral outdoor space at night, and from thence the production moves to the main setting.

All of the action takes place out of doors in either Olivia's

(Caroline Langrishe) or Orsino's (Christopher Ravenscroft) garden. Their estates seem to be adjacent since Olivia's garden remains in view during scenes filmed on Orsino's terrace. Hers includes the grave of her brother and her father, to which she carries a rose (and Malvolio a wreath) on her first entrance. There is, too, a chaise-longue with a grandfather clock next to it. The time has stopped at twenty-five to three. This is neither explained nor referred to, but might have been the moment when one of the deaths occurred. Sir Toby (James Saxon) flips open the gravestone at the beginning of Act II, scene iii, to retrieve a bottle of sack.

The overall impact is one of winter festivity. There is a touch of frost throughout, a nip in the air, and it occasionally snows. A Christmas theme is introduced. At II.iii.79 the late-night revellers sing 'The Twelve Days of Christmas' (drunkenly forgetting the gifts brought on the seventh and sixth days), just before Malvolio enters. A decorated Christmas tree is brought onto the stage by Sir Toby, Sir Andrew (James Simmons) and Fabian (Shaun Prendergast) at the beginning of Act II, scene v. This becomes the box tree to hide behind, and the place where the letter is left (like an extra decoration), and the tree remains on the set for the rest of the production. Later, there are parcels under it.

The costuming suggests a late nineteenth-century setting. Fabian (who becomes a silent but involved presence in I.v and II.iii) is portrayed as a well-dressed gentlemanly servant. Maria (Abigail McKern) is portrayed as a housemaid (she first appears sweeping the front steps of Olivia's house). A cunning Sir Toby and a consistently wan-looking Sir Andrew remain well dressed throughout, with an aristocratic comportment. For the duel, Sir Andrew changes into full military period uniform. Malvolio (Richard Briers) appears in a Scrooge-like nightgown (with a Wee Willy Winkie sleeping hat), carrying a candelabrum, to interrupt the revels in Act II, scene iii, and looking like Laurence Olivier in John Gielgud's 1955 production. Briers sports a particularly inane grin during his attempts to woo Olivia, and appears dirty and utterly broken at the end. His last line is cried from off-stage, as an irrecoverable distance between him and the rest of Olivia's court grows.

Feste (Anton Lesser) appears as an alcoholic Bohemian figure, just a little too well kept to be a down and out. Complete with earring, fingerless gloves, collarless shirt, long, scruffy hair, and hip flask, he is poised always to be sharp and satirical, encourages drinking, and has an anachronistic air of the mid-1980s punk about him. Just after his entrance in Act II, scene iii, he produces from the inside of his long top coat four flute glasses, into which Fabian pours champagne for everyone. His quixotically gnomic behaviour leads him to crumple up the rose Olivia takes to the grave, on 'so beauty's a flower' (I.v.47), and read Orsino's palm for his speech beginning 'Now the melancholy god protect thee' (II.iv.72–7). The second verse of 'O mistress mine' is introverted and melancholy, and seems to offer a personalized excuse for Feste's nastiness.

A full text is used, to which the cast bring fine voice, as well as nuances to the dramatic poetry. When Orsino talks of 'a bank of violets' he is able to convey an aural suggestion of '*viola*-ets'. Feste feels every bit of the insult from Malvolio, who emphasizes '*set* kind of fools', and Feste himself manages to sound strangely prophetic (if one already knows the story) for the line 'the fool shall look to the madman' (I.v.129–30), which is immediately followed by the entrance of Malvolio. Frances Barber's crisp and piquant delivery as Viola brings humour – 'No, good *swabber*' (I.v.195) sounds incredibly cheeky – and allows for the portrayal of a clear-sighted personal journey throughout. She speaks directly into the camera for her soliloquies and asides. The camera shows Olivia falling hopelessly in love with her during the 'willow cabin' speech. There are no complexities of desire or self-conscious clevernesses of interpretation at work in this production, but its many fine balances of mood, characterization and poetic diction make it highly worthwhile.

Trevor Nunn's quickly paced, strongly cast 1996 film version depicts a pervasive autumnal tone throughout: muted colours, unapologetically darkened interiors, apples being harvested in the orchard. There is a distinct and ever-present melancholy ready to break through into the comedy. Filmed partly on location on the Cornish coast, it continually reminds the viewer of the sweeping presence and metaphorical power of the ocean; of time passing, a reminder of the futility of human endeavour, and mortality.

The film resonates with novelistic detail, in which Nunn's theatre productions are also keenly interested. At the beginning a background story is established through a prologue written by Nunn in iambic pentameter. Viola (Imogen Stubbs) and Sebastian (Steven Mackintosh) appear as on-board cabaret entertainers. Both twins wear a moustache and appear as female impersonators. After the shipwreck separates them, and before the opening titles, Viola is established as a threatened fugitive in Illyria (hence her disguise), Feste (Ben Kingsley) as a wise observer, Olivia as mourning for her brother (and the empathy that Viola feels for her as a result), and we are shown the intricacies of Viola's disguise. She uses clothes from the wreckage, cuts her long hair, binds her breasts flat, places a rolled-up piece of material in her trousers to give the impression of a penis, practises a masculine walk with the sea captain, and deepens her voice by screaming loudly from a cliff.

Other examples of Nunn's fine detail include Malvolio sitting up late reading a magazine called *Amour* as he gradually gets agitated by the below-stairs revellers. Maria (Imelda Staunton) notices his yellow stockings first during his reprimand and we may perceive the seed of her plot being planted. Malvolio corrects the sundial against his watch as he enters for the eavesdropping scene (a piece of business harking back to Donald Sinden's 1969 RSC performance), and is prompted to speak about Olivia when he sees a statue of a naked woman in the garden. Sebastian has a copy of 'Baedeker's Illyria from Randazzo to Mistretta' for Act III, scene ii, and Feste enters wearing Malvolio's toupee for his final moment of mocking 'Why, "Some are born great . . ." ' (V.i.361–7).

Relationships are carefully detailed. Sir Toby (Mel Smith) lets sunlight into the room and settles down to play differently rhythmic dance tunes for Sir Andrew (Richard E. Grant) in Act I, scene iii. They are stopped in their tracks by Nigel Hawthorne's surly Malvolio, who has just been casting his beady eye over Maria and the kitchen arrangements. Nunn adopts an Edwardian setting so that the aristocratic distinctions and the hierarchy of the servants can be clearly defined. Cesario and Orsino (Toby Stephens) suggest a homoerotic subtext. He calls her to wash his back in the bath; the two of them move close together and almost kiss during Feste's 'Come away death'. Maria is presented as an important nurturer for Feste and gives him food in the kitchen in Act I, scene v. Intimacy between Olivia and Feste is also established in I.v. Just after her friendly warning 'Now you see, sir, how your fooling grows old and people dislike it' (I.v.105–6) she weeps and goes to him for comfort, resting her head on his breast. Maria and Sir Toby's relationship is carefully plotted throughout. There are tears in her eyes as she looks across to him in the kitchen during the singing of 'O mistress mine', and she is disappointed when he does not follow her to bed after 'For this night, to bed' (II.iii.163). During Feste's song 'I am gone, sir' he sees Toby and Maria through a church window, about to be married; Olivia and Sebastian are kissing in the churchyard at the same time.

Throughout, Nunn freely adapts and rearranges the text for the sake of pacing and visual variation. Words thought to be too difficult are changed, for example 'breeches' for 'gaskins' (I.v.23), and 'learn' for 'con' (I.v.166). Orsino says 'O, she that hath a heart of that fine frame / To pay this debt of love but to a brother' (I.i.32–3) directly to Cesario (who is not supposed to be present); it prompts her to call to mind an image of her drowning brother. Feste's final song is set against his watching people leave Olivia's household. Sir Andrew illustrates 'a foolish thing', Antonio 'knaves and thieves' (calling to mind his piracy). Sir Toby and Maria drive past in their carriage for 'alas, to wive'; Malvolio's leaving illustrates 'tosspots'. As the final credits roll, the two aristocratic couples are dancing at a wedding feast, and we all get to see Viola in her 'woman's weeds'.

Tim Supple's 2003 film was first shown on Channel 4 television and billed as an 'enthralling comedy'. This uncompromisingly modern and multi-cultural interpretation is full of clever interpretative choices, which are sufficiently integrated to avoid becoming mere conceits. The initial exposition of the shipwreck is deliberately mysterious. Images of a brutal separation are spliced into Orsino's (Chiwetel Ejiotor) opening speech. Viola (Parminder Nagra) is taken away from Sebastian (Ronny Jhutti) by men with guns, who soon after ignite the space between the twins. A few moments later, they appear together on board a ship, surrounded by other Indian immigrants. A man approaches them with some papers and talks to Sebastian. No shipwreck is shown, and we are left to rely on the Sea Captain's report of it (I.ii.5–16). Viola's Illyria is a dockland area somewhere along the Thames.

The strongly Indian casting allows a restrained tone of 'Bollywood' into the overarching filmic vision, and there are moments of magic realism. Sebastian and Viola disappear into thin air as they are about to jump through a starlit window near the beginning. Orsino's palace is abstract in its location and looks out onto a panorama of ocean and horizon, which contributes the sound of the waves as a persistent symbol of his desires. There is, for example, a glorious sunrise in Act II, scene iv, when he decides that Viola must return to Olivia (Claire Price). When Viola first hears of Orsino he briefly appears on the screen like Cupid drawing a bow. A few moments later this surprising image is borne out: Orsino looks the same and really is practising his archery. The practice of inserting such images also allows us to glimpse Olivia's father and brother (from the wrecked car which flashes onto the screen we can infer how he died), as well as Sebastian of Messaline at II.ii.15 (who looks ducal and was shot dead). Olivia turns to see her brother playing the piano during the moment it takes for Maria (Maureen Beattie) to fetch Cesario. In Supple's Illyria, made up of abstract and real locations, anything can happen.

Sir Toby (David Troughton) and Sir Andrew (Richard Bremmer) inhabit a cellar-like space. Sir Toby is first seen looking at photographs of Olivia's dead brother. In Act I, scene v, when he appears in Olivia's chapel he seems suddenly overwhelmed by the religious symbols (explicitly Roman Catholic), making his 'Give me faith, say I' (I.v.122–3) a literal cry from the heart of a lost soul. He drinks out of a bottle, but decants Sir Andrew's allocation into a glass. He plays a heavy metal record version of 'Hold thy peace, thou knave' for Sir Andrew to dance to at the end of Act I, scene iii. The dartboard on the wall of their cellar reminds us of Orsino's romantic archery; for Sir Toby and Sir Andrew, though, love is a cruder kind of sport. Their 'caterwauling' (II.iii.68) is Feste's (Zubin Varla) version of 'Hold thy peace' on a synthesizer while Sir Toby plays it on an electric guitar and Sir Andrew bangs on the water pipes. Maria interrupts by unplugging the leads, on her entrance. Sir Andrew's 'I was adored once, too' (II.iii.169) is delivered as though it were a sudden recollection of something he has all but forgotten. The eavesdropping scene is done by them spying on Malvolio (Michael Maloney) with the help of a video camera. Although this takes away any threat of them being discovered by him, their heightened and unrestrained gratification as they stare into the television screen makes it seem as though they were watching a pornographic film.

The nexus of relationships around Viola suffers because she appears too feminine throughout. She is hard-edged during her first meeting with Olivia, which makes Olivia's desire for her entirely one-directional. Between Viola and Orsino there is more ambiguity. She massages his back while he is in his steam bath (which is similar to the parallel scenario in Trevor Nunn's film) and gets to see him completely naked a moment later. Orsino fondles her front shirt buttons on 'all is semblative a woman's part' (I.iv.34). Later, Orsino's inner self is shown to separate from where he is sitting and arise to embrace Viola for her lines 'I am all the daughters of my father's house / And all the brothers, too' (II.iv.120–1).

The cultural otherness of Viola and Sebastian (they are Indian, Orsino black African, Olivia white) is reiterated through occasional moments of Indian dialect. Shakespeare's words then appear as subtitles, for example, between Antonio (Andrew Kazamin), who the film suggests is an agent for illegal immigrants, and Sebastian. On being reunited, Viola and Sebastian also share a few words in their native language.

Malvolio (Michael Maloney) is portrayed with great tenderness and hardly any absurdity. He exercises a tempered authority over Sir Toby in Act II, scene iii, without seeming pompous, pointing up the alliterative 'coziers' catches' (II.iii.85), and is calmly prepared for Sir Toby's retaliating insults. The smiling that he practises in Act II, scene v, is done with a careful conviction of its purpose, and his response of 'To bed? Ay, sweetheart, and I'll come to thee' to Olivia (III.iii.28–9) is delivered with an utter seriousness of hope and confessional gratitude. His imprisonment is especially cruel. Both hands are bound against the opposite walls of a cage-like cupboard in Sir Toby's cellar and a bag is tied over his head. His rages are ferocious as he kicks against the metal cell door. Olivia and the others go to see him there at the end. Malvolio leaves with quiet dignity on his last line.

In the final moments, Olivia sees the photographs of her brother in Sir Toby's album and her mood suddenly changes as she seems to catch a glimpse of a better world which she has lost forever. She exits sobbing, on 'He hath been most notoriously abused' (V.i.369), and Orsino follows to offer her comfort on her terrace beneath the stars. After Orsino's lines to Viola about her becoming her 'master's mistress', the final line before Feste's song (sung as the credits roll) goes to Olivia. She turns to Viola, for 'A sister, you are she' (V.i.317). Throughout, Tim Supple freely rearranges the text and brings a great sense of mystery and visual richness to his film. He manages finely to balance romantic comedy with an overarching sense of a grittier, harsher-edged reality: a magic realist fantasy from which there is no escape.

5 Critical Assessments

There is a great and ever-growing mass of critical work surrounding *Twelfth Night*. Careful engagement with other critical voices is a way of sharing and exploring the views of a whole range of readers over the centuries. Doing so can help develop one's own knowledge, understanding and, most importantly, enjoyment of the play. This chapter presents an overview of diverse approaches, with the acknowledgement that the bulk of Shakespeare criticism has been produced within the last fifty years. The main principle of selection has been a keenly felt duty to present the reader with some of the best representative work available for further consultation and study. The three sections – 'Character', 'Theatre' and 'Comedy and desire' – present the material chronologically within their own thematic arrangement. Where possible the references given are to anthologies of criticism, which are more readily available for further exploration.

Character

Leonard Digges's eulogy in the First Folio of 1623 praised Shakespeare's powerful and naturalistic depiction of characters. The critical tradition of analysing the personalities of Shakespeare's creations as though they were real people has continued ever since. From Samuel Johnson's great preface to his 1765 edition of Shakespeare, in which he relates the individual characters of Sir Andrew, Malvolio and Olivia to the overall comic effect, the study of Shakespeare's characters has become one of the most dominant critical acts. William Hazlitt was influential in encouraging this kind of reading in his *Characters of Shakespeare's Plays* in 1817:

The great and secret charm of *Twelfth Night* is the character of Viola. Much as we like catches and cakes and ale, there is something that we like better. We have friendship for Sir Toby; we patronise Sir Andrew; we have an understanding with the Clown, a sneaking kindness for Maria and her rogueries; we feel a regard for Malvolio, and sympathise with his gravity, his smiles, his cross garters, his yellow stockings, and imprisonment in the stocks. But there is something that excites in us a stronger feeling than all this – it is Viola's confession of her love.   (Palmer, *Casebook*, pp. 31–2)

Hazlitt's observations not only reflect the sensibilities of his age, but are also revealing about the performances he saw (with Malvolio being put into the stocks, for example). Hazlitt's tone in the above extract is also one of licensing and allowance: appropriate in relation to a play about a feast of misrule and authorized misbehaviour.

Extracts from character criticism from the mid- to late nineteenth century are printed as an appendix in Horace Howard Furness's monumental New Variorum edition of *Twelfth Night* (1901). Anna Jameson is representative of what British theatre in the nineteenth century tended to bring to portrayals of Shakespeare's heroine:

The feminine cowardice of Viola, which will not allow her even to affect a courage becoming her attire, her horror at the idea of drawing a sword, is very natural and characteristic; and it produces a most humorous effect, even at the moment it charms and interests us.   (in Furness, New Variorum, p. 392)

Jameson's seminal and influential study *Characteristics of Women, Moral, Poetical, and Historical* (1832) also relates to performance, and constitutes one of the first female voices ever to write about Viola. In 1851–2 Mary Cowden Clarke published the imaginative three-volume collection of short stories *Girlhood of Shakespeare's Heroines*, each of which ends with the first lines spoken by the character in Shakespeare's play. Other significant contributions to the analysis of character include G. G. Gervinus, who, in 1850, made observations about Orsino – 'a tender, poetic soul . . . more in love with his love, than with his mistress' – which have long been a critical common-place (in Furness, New Variorum, p. 379). By the end of the nineteenth century W. Winter, in his *Shadows of the Stage* (1895), combined further the dramatic quality of the Violas he had seen in performance with Viola as a body of text to be interpreted: 'Rosalind [in *As You Like It*] is a woman. Viola is a poem.' Winter praised Ada Rehan's performance of Viola for playing her as 'a woman of deep sensibility . . . permitting a wistful sadness to glimmer through the gauze of kindly vivacity' (in Furness, *New Variorum*, pp. 394 and 395).

The pioneering dramaturgy of Konstantin Stanislavsky at the end of the nineteenth century encouraged critics and theatre practitioners to focus more on dramatic characters' imaginary inner lives. His work as a director at the Moscow Arts Theatre explored ways of connecting an actor's subjective feelings to the physical and verbal impact of a role. Stanislavsky produced *Twelfth Night* in 1896, with revivals in 1899 and 1917. A. C. Bradley (whose important book, *Shakespearean Tragedy* appeared in 1904) is a powerful exponent of character criticism who greatly influenced twentieth-century Shakespeare studies. There is an article about Feste published in 1916. Bradley is interested in an all-seeing Feste, a fool whose expression of integrity is done as much for himself as for anyone else: 'We never laugh at Feste. . . . He enters, and at once we know that Maria's secret is no secret to him.' Bradley's Feste demands our sympathy, 'his soul is in the song', and, since he can see into the other characters' minds and sense their emotions, he becomes a correlative for Shakespeare himself, 'looking down from an immeasurable height on the mind of the public and the noble' (Wells, *Critical Essays*, pp. 17, 19 and 23). Bradley's is an early psychoanalytic reading of the role, which relates Feste to Shakespeare's own unconscious. Sigmund Freud, who began reading Shakespeare when he was eight, and whose influential and radical works began to appear in English from the mid-1920s, used Shakespeare's plays to help illustrate his theories of the unconscious. Stanislavsky, Bradley and Freud together represent a crucial moment of development in the understanding and exploration of what we mean by 'character'.

John Masefield's 1911 survey of the plays represents the kind of criticism which deduces an underlying moral purpose from the way Shakespeare's characters behave. For example:

Malvolio is mocked out of sentiment by the knowledge that other minds

have seen his mind. He has not the happiness to be rewarded with love
... but he has the alternative of hate, which is as active a passion and as
real. All three [Orsino, Olivia and Malvolio] are roused to activity by the
coming of something real into their lives; and all three, in coming to the
active state, cease to be interesting and beautiful and pathetic.

Shakespeare's abundant power created beings who look before and
after, even while they keep vigorous a passionate present. . . . Within two
minutes of the talk of the woman who died of love he showed
Contemplation making a rare turkey-cock [II.v.28–9] of the one wise man
in his play.   (Masefield, *William Shakespeare*, pp. 141–2 and p. 143)

Masefield's moral criticism survived even the First World War. J. B.
Priestley produced an absorbing essay about 'The Illyrians' a decade
later (1925) which with great ease draws together much earlier
comment and combines it with essayistic playfulness and imagination (Wells, *Critical Essays*, pp. 1–16). Twenty-five years on, and five
years after the Second World War (1950), John W. Draper published
a singularly in-depth study of *Twelfth Night*'s characters (*The Twelfth
Night of Shakespeare's Audience*), whom he attempts to historicize in
terms of historical setting and reception.

Today's criticism tends to eschew any notion of identifiable 'characters' and sees Shakespeare's roles as politically and historically
inscribed textual constructs. However, some modern criticism does
still continue to read for character and this practice is certainly alive
and well in the teaching of Shakespeare in secondary schools. This
interpretative and critical act can be enlivened and refreshed by a
consideration of performance. After all, actors are continually practising character criticism.

Theatre

John Bell's theatrical edition of Shakespeare (1763) includes illuminating notes by Francis Gentleman which suggest how the plays
were produced, acted and received in the eighteenth century. *Twelfth
Night* is in volume 5. Bell's two illustrations are of Malvolio, clearly
the comic and dramatic highpoint. The introduction notices that:

Malvolio's ridiculous self-sufficiency is displayed in a most masterly manner: Sir Toby and Sir Andrew keep pace with him; and Viola, though romantic in her love, is delicately sustained. . . . Action must render [the play] more pleasing than perusal.   (p. 295)

The cast lists of the Drury Lane and Covent Garden theatres appear at the front. The notes suggest casting and probably recall actual performers. For example, Orsino's role 'may be supported by a second rate actor' (p. 297), a Sir Toby needs 'jollity of features, figure and expression' (p. 300), Maria 'nothing but ease, and a tolerable person' (p. 300), Olivia 'possessed of beauty, figure, and grace, with sensibility of speech' (p. 306). Malvolio's appearance in the yellow stockings is 'truly ridiculous [. . .] requiring great peculiarity of look and action' (p. 335). The Sir Topaz scene, which has come to be regarded as cruel, is 'truly comic, and an eccentric flight of warm imagination' (p. 347). The notes also reveal popular abridgements of the time, which include I.i.9–15 and II.iv.19–21. Of Viola's speech beginning 'A blank, my lord' (II.iv.110–18) it is noted that Shakespeare never surpassed this speech for 'picturesque beauty' (p. 320).

Charles Lamb's 'On Some of the Old Actors' (*Essays of Elia*, 1823) includes a passing reference to a production of *Twelfth Night* which he saw in 1792 when he was just seventeen. The tone of voice Lamb adopts seems much older than its author's forty-eight years. It is unashamedly essayistic, nostalgic, and sentimental. Lamb's self-exploratory tone combined with his own view of this time as a golden age of theatre disrupts any sense of his readers gaining a direct access to what the production was like. Robert Bensley's Malvolio, according to other reports, was much more straightforwardly in the comic vein than Lamb remembers. But Lamb makes several valuable observations about the possibilities for *Twelfth Night* in performance.

For Lamb, Malvolio can be performed with 'a richness and a dignity' (contextualized by Lamb recalling Bensley as both Hotspur in *Henry IV Part One* and Iago in *Othello*). Lamb believes that 'Malvolio is not essentially ludicrous. He becomes comic but by accident', and that Bensley brought 'a kind of tragic interest' to the role (Wells, *Critical Essays*, pp. 51, 52 and 54). Lamb's recollection of Dorothea Jordan's Viola is intended to celebrate the actor in her prime, before her voice changed with age. In so doing, Lamb gives a theatrical reading of a particular moment:

> when she had declared her sister's history to be a 'blank', and that she 'never told her love' [II.iv.110], there was a pause, as if the story had ended – and then the image of the 'worm in the bud' came up as a new suggestion – and the heightened image of 'Patience' still followed after that, as by some growing (and not mechanical process), thought springing up after thought, I would almost say, as they were watered by her tears.   (Wells, *Critical Essays*, p. 50)

The Olivia of Mrs Powel sported with and then dismissed her Feste (played by Dicky Suett with 'a loose and shambling gait [and] a slippery tongue'); the Sir Andrew of Mr Dodd 'surpassed all others' in expressing the 'slowness of apprehension' (Wells, *Critical Essays*, pp. 57 and 54).

Theatre reviews will always be inflected by the personal interests of the reporter, but they remain one of the most valuable resources with which to consider and reflect upon past productions. In 1944, Arthur Colby Sprague illustrated a brief discussion of some major points in the play with reference to productions from 1763 to 1901, in *Shakespeare and the Actors* (extract included in Wells, *Critical Essays*, pp. 39–48).

The breakthrough production of the twentieth century was Harley Granville-Barker's at the Savoy in 1912. This stylized and innovatory Illyria presented what was understood to be a truthfulness of characterization with a dexterously spoken text. In his brief preface to an edition of the play published to accompany his production, Granville-Barker comments on the spareness of *Twelfth Night*'s Elizabethan staging, his own conviction that the action would have been continuous (intervals, Granville-Barker permits after II.iii and IV.i, if necessary), 'the half-Italianised court of Elizabeth' (borne out in his own production), and the need to speak the verse quickly (Granville-Barker, *Prefaces*, pp. 27 and 31). His original but cursory observations on characterization were genuinely illuminating. Sir Toby is a gentleman who wants the security and power resulting from Sir Andrew marrying his niece Olivia, neither Fabian nor Feste is young, and Antonio is 'an exact picture of an Elizabethan seaman-adventurer'. Granville-Barker is revealing about his period's stage portrayals of Viola: 'it is common practice for actresses of Viola to seize every chance of reminding the audience that they are girls dressed up' (Granville-Barker, *Prefaces*, p. 29), and he urges us to recall that the role was originally played by a boy.

His remarks on Sir Andrew being a credible and perfect gentleman (Granville-Barker, *Prefaces*, p. 30) were endorsed by Peter Hall in his own preface to the Folio Society edition. He refers to Sir Andrew as one of Elizabethan literature's pretentious 'gentlemen bumpkins' (Hall, 'Introduction', p. 8). Both Granville-Barker and Hall want Sir Andrew's comedy to arise from the audience taking him seriously. Granville-Barker's balanced review of Jacques Copeau's famous French production (1914; revived 1921) is as sensitively engaged a description of dramatic nuance in speech, movement and on-stage relationships as one could wish for (included in Wells, *Critical Essays*, pp. 71–8).

The occasion for Virginia Woolf's review of Tyrone Guthrie's production in 1933 is as interesting as what she has to observe. The press had demurred and Woolf was acutely aware that she had to write optimistically for her friends John Maynard Keynes and his ballet-dancing wife Lydia Lopokova (who played Olivia). Woolf's modernist sensibilities shine through the result. Part meditation about the tension of reading the play and seeing it, and part review, Woolf's writing conveys the happy melancholy of *Twelfth Night*. She begins with an elegiac landscape reminiscent of John Keats's 'Ode to Autumn'. Her haunting review conveys the importance of the play's linguistic music for a reader as much as for a theatre audience.

> There is a good deal to be said for reading *Twelfth Night* . . . in a garden, with no sound but the thud of an apple falling to the earth, or of the wind ruffling the branches of the trees. For one thing there is time – time not only to hear 'the sweet sound that breathes upon a bank of violets' but to unfold the implications of that very subtle speech as the Duke winds into the nature of love. There is time, too, to make a note in the margin; time to wonder at the queer jingles like 'that live in her; when liver, brain, and heart' . . . 'and of a foolish knight that you brought in one night' and to

ask oneself whether it was from them that was born the lovely 'And what
should I do in Illyria? My brother he is in Elysium.' . . . From the echo of
one word is born another word, for which reason, perhaps the play seems
as we read it to tremble perpetually on the brink of music.   (Wells,
Critical Essays, p. 79)

A breakthrough for the study of the theatrical life of *Twelfth Night*
came in 1966 with John Russell Brown's *Shakespeare's Plays in
Performance*, a landmark study in the tradition of Granville-Barker,
which encouraged and developed an emerging scholarly interest in
theatre practice through the 1970s to the present day. Brown reiterated the question 'What is the effect?' rather than 'What is the meaning?' of a Shakespearian play (Brown, *Plays*, p. 14), and presents case
studies to explore issues including linguistic rhythms, subtext (illustrated by Act II, scene iv), comic business, and stage pictures. An
appendix gives advice on the resources and methodology of theatre
research. His chapter 'Directions for *Twelfth Night*' cites interpretative
choices from some major 1950s productions in Stratford-upon-
Avon and London, as well as emphasizing how close attention to the
text can be richly suggestive for stage design. Above all, theatre is
about discovery. There is never a definitive production, only degrees
of considered and informed definition. In 2001 Brown edited the play
for the Applause Shakespeare series, the aim of which is to present
the theatrical life of the text – its pauses, sounds, and movement –
through a performance commentary.

A careful study of a landmark production is exemplified by
Stanley Wells's 1976 descriptive essay on John Barton's RSC production in 1969–72. Wells contextualizes Barton's directorial process in
relation to his university and artistic background before giving a
detailed account of the effect of the production, its interpretative
choices and emotional impact. The essay conveys the production's
'fusion of tones' (Wells, *Royal Shakespeare*, p. 49) by noticing, for example, the use of sound effects (birdsong, waves breaking), the poetic
acting of Judi Dench as Viola (her voice breaking on 'and all the *brothers* too', II.iv.121; 'Tempests are kind, and salt waves fresh in love!' was
a moment of faith and hope pointed by lighting and sound, III.iv.375),
the wistful melancholy of Maria's attraction to Sir Toby, and the

exuberance of the singing in Act II, scene iii ('O Mistress Mine' was clearly an old favourite and Shakespeare's 'O the twelfth day of December' prompted a burst of 'The Twelve Days of Christmas'). In all, Wells notices 'a beauty of communication, of sympathy, under-standing, and compassion . . . a Chekhovian quality' in Barton's production (Wells, *Royal Shakespeare*, p. 62).

Anton Chekhov's name is often invoked to describe productions of *Twelfth Night*. The director Richard Eyre's praise of Chekhov's 'qual-ity of even-handedly creating characters who seem to exist indepen-dently of their maker' (*Guardian Review*, 5 March 2005, p. 18) is the kind of remark which often identifies a similar trait in Shakespeare's own genius. For a modern audience, that trait can be identified in the opposite direction, too. The comic collection of eccentric individuals in *Twelfth Night*, and a pervasive melancholy often resonant in productions, can make it seem, especially in performance, Chekhovian in tone. The director Trevor Nunn praised Peter Hall's 1958 RSC production for being 'Chekhovian'. In 1981, the critic Ralph Berry explained that the pervasive use of the adjective in relation to *Twelfth Night* relates to Chekhov's impact on twentieth-century comedy, because Chekhov 'is the father of Beckett and Pinter' (Berry, *Changing Styles*, pp. 113 and 117). That *Twelfth Night* has become Chekhovian is mainly because of the dramatic tastes and dynamics of productions from the middle of the twentieth century onwards.

Two important contributions relate back to Barton's 1969 produc-tion. The first is John Barton's own *Playing Shakespeare* (1984): a televi-sion series of exploratory workshops, as well as a book. One chapter provides an in-depth account of how Shakespeare's text works in Act II, scene iv, its rhythms as prompts for stresses and pauses in perfor-mance. The actors working on Viola and Orsino are Judi Dench and Richard Pasco, who played the roles in Barton's production. The second is a detailed account by Donald Sinden, who played Malvolio, which is included in *Players of Shakespeare 1* (Brockbank, 1985). This is a moment-by-moment description of what he saw and did as the drama unfolded, and conveys a sense of how he spoke the lines. Sinden rates each laugh his performance was able to generate on a scale of one to nine, and there are even illustrations of Maria's letter and what it looked like as he unfolded it.

Jean E. Howard's *Shakespeare's Art of Orchestration: Stage Technique and Audience Response* (1984) offers a moment-by-moment, aurally and visually sensitive account of *Twelfth Night* as it unfolds in performance:

> the play is crafted to tamper with the satisfaction of some very basic theatrical appetites – a desire for movement, happening, clear speeches eventuating in insight and action . . . that we feel in the theater as pent-up kinetic energy begging for release.   (Bloom, *William Shakespeare's 'Twelfth Night'*, pp. 107–8)

Howard's study was followed a year later by Lois Potter's *Twelfth Night: Text and Performance* (1985), produced to encourage further the dialogue between the academy and the theatre. Potter's insightful and illustrated guide includes a detailed exploration of the final scene, gives a survey of eighteenth- and nineteenth-century productions, and considers four productions in detail: the 1969 and 1974 RSC productions, the 1979 Leicester Haymarket production and the one staged at the Berkeley Shakespeare Festival in 1981–2. Potter's study, and the series of which it was a part, were made possible by the kind of critical enquiry outlined above, represented by Brown, Wells, and Barton. Although the distinction the series makes between 'Text' and 'Performance' makes for a convenient but divisive structure, Potter's critical practice admirably relates the two fictionally enabling areas together.

Three other accounts by actors include insights into playing Viola and Olivia. Zoë Wanamaker gives an insightful and candid account of key moments in John Caird's 1983 RSC production, for example the smell of her brother on his clothes she wears, and the play as a 'chamber piece' (Jackson and Smallwood, *Players of Shakespeare* 2, pp. 86 and 83). Emma Fielding blends an accumulative character study with her own theatrical process in Ian Judge's 1994 RSC production. She conveys an impression of how the role developed during the stretch of the production, sharing insights along the way. For example, she comments on the struggles between male and female sexuality in her relationship with Orsino, and how the production was 'punctuated by kisses' between the different protagonists (Fielding,

Twelfth Night, p. 44). Zoë Waites and Matilda Ziegler provide a useful account of the developing relationship between Viola and Olivia in Lindsay Posner's 2001 RSC production. This includes five pages on Act I, scene v alone, detailing the vulnerability and protection on both sides (Olivia's veil being all-important for the first part). The two of them shared two controversial kisses. The first, on 'Love sought is good, but unsought is better' (III.i.154), a welcome moment of 'sexual curiosity' on both sides. The second came just before they exited together at the end of the final scene, an 'enjoyably provocative' affirmation of mutual self-knowledge (Smallwood, *Players of Shakespeare 5*, pp. 69 and 73). These three descriptions serve intimately to open up the play with regard to the different dramatic and emotional energies that actors bring to it.

Two contrasting books by directors of *Twelfth Night* provide rich material relating to the interpretative choices made in actual performances. *Directors' Shakespeare: Approaches to 'Twelfth Night'* (1990) presents a series of discussions chaired and edited by the *Guardian* theatre critic Michael Billington with four RSC directors: John Barton (1969), Terry Hands (1979), John Caird (1983) and Bill Alexander (1987). Arranged under headings such as 'What kind of play?', 'The Choice of Period', 'The Problem of Viola's First Scene', and 'The Laughter and the Pain', the discussions were recorded and are presented in the form of a five-way conversation. The pleasure for the reader is the gradual unfolding of specialist views; there are lively disagreements, and practical solutions. The discussions are also riddled with often impressionistic theories, and the quality of listening among the speakers fluctuates. But the book is rich in opinion, both original and commonplace, and illustrates perfectly the restless exploration of practical theatre.

Michael Pennington's *Twelfth Night: A User's Guide* (2002) attempts to be more definitive in the way it tackles the play in performance. Pennington directed a production for the English Shakespeare Company in 1991. His companionable and unashamedly sentimental account is partly a celebration of that (and its world tour), but is mainly a scene-by-scene description of how the play works in a theatre, shot through with personal reflections about the then current affairs, and Shakespearian study more generally.

Pennington's valuable observations seem to be inextricably tied to his own production and are neither open ended nor exploratory. His commentary assumes an authoritative tone throughout, which paradoxically at once evades and makes present the inescapably ephemeral nature of the theatrical process. But Pennington writes beautifully and his account brings his extensive knowledge and experience as an actor and director to bear on *Twelfth Night*.

Comedy and desire

The subtitle for this section could appropriately be *Or What You Will*. 'Will' in Shakespeare's period, as well as possibly alluding to the male and female genitalia, could more generally mean 'desire'. Shakespeare's alternative title invites its audiences to position (or to find) themselves in relation to the play, to interpret it in their own image: such is the desire of every critical act. Discussions of the play's genre (often characterized by on-going attempts to theorize about why and how Shakespeare wrote comedies) are the result of critics' desires to net *Twelfth Night*, to convey the sense of its wholeness, to possess it through interpretation, and to influence the thinking of others. It is appropriate that the underlying comic dynamics of the play have ensured its position as a key text for critics interested in gender and sexuality. Critical desires of all kinds and from all perspectives continue to develop as new questions are asked. What follows includes examples of critics willing the play to mean what they desire, as well as willing the desire in the play to reflect the critics' own interests.

In 1766, Thomas Tyrwhitt implausibly argued that *Twelfth Night* was Shakespeare's last play, written in 1614 (Furness, New Variorum, pp. viii–ix). Although Edmond Malone dated it late (1607) in his 1790 edition, Tyrwhitt's argument held sway. It was affirmed by the great German critic August Wilhelm Von Schlegel in his *Lectures on Dramatic Art and Literature* (1808–11, first translated into English in 1815). The Romantic essayist Leigh Hunt's views, expressed in *The Examiner* (November 1820), are summed up by Gary Taylor:

Leigh Hunt, assuring his readers that 'Twelfth Night was that last work of Shakespeare' marvelled at 'what a good natured play' it was; Shakespeare's 'last thoughts' of the world were 'kind and social', dwelling upon 'the humours of good fellowship and the young trustingness of love'.   (Taylor, *Reinventing Shakespeare*, p. 157)

The sense of the play being an apotheosis of Shakespearian comedy continued through the nineteenth century. In 1862, the German scholar F. Kreyssig found there comic perfection:

That saying of Goethe: 'That in every finished work of Shakespeare there could be found a central idea', here finds its justification in fullest measure. Let it be supposed that Shakespeare had set himself the task to show, within the limit of one treatment, like a recapitulation, every combination of comedies in one single comedy, and it would not be difficult to prove that in *Twelfth Night* the task had been successfully accomplished.   (in Furness, New Variorum, p. 381)

That 'the play is a culmination of virtually every aspect of the comedies that come before it' is a view which is echoed 141 years later by William C. Carroll (Wells and Orlin, *Shakespeare: An Oxford Guide*, p. 186). Scholarship now locates *Twelfth Night* comfortably in Shakespeare's middle period (1601), but there it sits as the last of his romantic comedies, pitched just before the bitterness of *Troilus and Cressida* (later the same year?) and the beginning of the great tragic period. It is understandable how so successful a Shakespearian combination of the comic with tragic undertones was understood to be a late achievement. The play being done, Feste's final song about the whole of a life in miniature, 'And we'll strive to please you every day', might also have encouraged the belief.

Looking for desire in the play used to be repressed. Emily Brontë's first-person narrator Mr Lockwood, in *Wuthering Heights* (1847), alludes to Viola's speech (II.iv.110) in chapter 1 to describe his own suppression of desire:

I 'never told my love' vocally; still, if looks have language, the merest idiot might have guessed I was head over ears; she understood me, at least, and looked a return – the sweetest of all imaginable looks – and what did I do? I confess it with shame – shrunk icily into myself.   (p. 48)

Lockwood's and Viola's suppression combine in Brontë's own, who initially hid (as did her sisters) her female identity with the androgynous pseudonym Ellis Bell. A French Shakespeare critic, E. Montégut, writing in 1867, is trembling on the brink of describing a love which dare not speak its name:

> What is to be said of Olivia but that her imagination, suddenly smitten, could go so far astray as to stifle in her the instinct which should have revealed to her that Viola was of her own sex? The friendship of Antonio for Sebastian, – a friendship which involves him in perils so easily foreseen, – is a sentiment exactly twin with the love of Olivia for Cesario–Viola. All dream, all are mad.   (Furness, New Variorum, p. 384)

The critical language for which Montégut seems to be reaching in this extract would remain repressed for at least another 120 years.

Repression (our early twenty-first century world likes to reflect back to us) was a hallmark of the 1950s. Representative criticism of the kinds of questions being raised from the late 1950s to the early 1980s are included in Stanley Wells's *Critical Essays*, and illustrate how far Shakespearian studies have changed and developed since then. L. G. Salingar (1958), C. L. Barber (1959), Harold Jenkins (1959), Bertrand Evans (1960) and A. S. Leggatt (1974) all attempt to describe the effect of the play as a whole, its distinctive features among Shakespeare's other comedies, its canonical place as a moment of creative and generic transition, and its structural arrangement. Salingar's opening questions – 'Is it, for example, a vindication of romance, or a description of romance? Is it mainly a love-story or a comedy of humours; "a poem of escape" or a realistic comment on economic security and prudential marriage?' (Wells, *Critical Essays*, p. 191) – are still being answered within current critical trends. Similarly, Harry Levin's 1976 exploration of how the main romantic elements relate to the comic sub-plot offers an anthropological reading, which has proved to be a popular feature of *Twelfth Night* criticism from the second half of the twentieth century:

> What we have been watching is a re-enactment of a timeless ritual, whose theatrical manifestation takes the obvious form of the villain foiled, and

whose deeper roots in folklore go back to the scapegoat cast into the outer darkness.

Levin goes on to describe Pieter Brueghel's painting *Battle between Carnival and Lent* and concludes that Shakespeare 'loaded his dice on the side of carnival . . . against the Lenten Malvolio, that prince of wet-blankets' (Wells, *Critical Essays*, p. 169).

It is indeed a relief to have moved on from what now seems like a stiflingly repressive critical climate, illustrated here by C. L. Barber's then innovatory *Shakespeare's Festive Comedy* (1959):

> The most fundamental distinction the play brings home to us is the difference between men and women. . . . Just as a saturnalian reversal of social roles need not threaten the social structure, but can serve instead to consolidate it, so a temporary, playful reversal of sexual roles can renew the meaning of the normal relation. One can add that with sexual as with other relations, it is when the normal is secure that playful aberration is benign. (Well, *Critical Essays*, p. 111)

Such a position would now be referred to as 'hetero-normative'. Although critical repression in relation to *Twelfth Night* disappeared slowly, the critical carnival was well under way by the early 1980s, and is still going strong. Coppélia Kahn must have seemed radical when she posited in *Man's Estate: Masculine Identity in Shakespeare* (1981) that, 'at some level, Cesario is a homosexual object choice for each of them [Orsino and Olivia]; at another a heterosexual one' (Bloom, *William Shakespeare's 'Twelfth Night'*, p. 44). But Kahn's conclusions at the end of her next page do not seem very different from Barber's from twenty years before:

> *Twelfth Night* traces the evolution of sexuality as related to identity, from the playful and conscious toying of youthful courtship, through a period of sexual confusion, to a final thriving in which swaggering is left behind and men and women truly know themselves through choosing the right mate. (Bloom, *William Shakespeare's 'Twelfth Night'*, p. 45)

It seems that sexual dissidence is all very well in youth, but there comes a time when everyone needs to settle down.

Stephen Greenblatt also revisited Barber in 'Fiction or Friction' as part of his *Shakespearian Negotiations: The Circulation of Social Energy in Renaissance England*, in 1988. It is an important piece because it takes up from where Kahn left off, and pointed to rich seams for future critics to mine. Some of the questions he seeks to address include the following:

> How does a play come to possess sexual energy? What happens when a body is translated from 'reality' to the stage or when a male actor is translated into the character of a woman?   (White, *New Casebooks*, p. 112)

The discussion he offers in answering them attempts 'to historicise Shakespearian sexual nature, restoring it to its relation of negotiation and exchange with other social discourses of the body' (White, *New Casebooks*, p. 98). One of his conclusions, via his typically pleasing circuitous route of sharing two Renaissance court cases involving cross-dressing and illicit sex, is that:

> more than any of his contemporaries, Shakespeare discovered how to use the erotic power that the theatre could appropriate, how to generate plots that would not block or ignore this power but draw it out, develop it, return it with interest, as it were, to the audience.   (White, *New Casebooks*, p. 113)

Greenblatt helped to establish an ever-developing critical trend, which traces desire as politically inscribed on the imagined and real bodies on the Renaissance stage. Dympna Callaghan's difficult 1993 article ' "And all is semblative a woman's part": Body Politics and *Twelfth Night*' presents a rigorous thesis which attempts to develop the historicization (and in part summarizes the critical development) of the Renaissance body which Greenblatt helped to inspire. Callaghan struggles to illustrate 'the absent-presence of female genitals' (White, *New Casebooks*, p. 133) in the idea of an authentic performance of *Twelfth Night* ('in other words, in [her] reading, what is at issue is not *whether it could be* represented, but *how it is* represented', p. 137). She concludes that although the 'biologically essential form – the cunt' (White, *New Casebooks*, p. 145) was literally absent in

Renaissance performance, it is present in many and perhaps unexpected metaphorical forms. Fifty-five years after Barber, sixteen years after Greenblatt and eleven years after Callaghan is Gail Kern Paster's *Humoring the Body: Emotions and the Shakespearian Stage* (2004), which offers a new and careful historicization of the Renaissance body in relation to Galen's theory of the four humours. Paster provides a way of reading which decodes, among other works, *Twelfth Night*'s language of the humours in relation to Shakespeare's depiction of human subjectivity.

Willing *Twelfth Night* to mean differently has involved careful and pleasurable decoding. John Kerrigan's 1997 'Secrecy and Gossip in *Twelfth Night*' is a subtle exposure of practices of concealment inscribed into the play's speech patterns, the presentation of sexual identity, political and social nuances, and the tension between 'employment and eroticism' (Kerrigan, *On Shakespeare*, pp. 90–1). Although not an exercise in an explicitly gay interpretation, Kerrigan's methodology exemplifies that of critics who seek for textual fissures, gaps from which meaning can be inferred through the referral to literary and dramatic contexts. So, in his discussion of Renaissance constructions of sexualities (which includes a fresh consideration of the 'eunuch' status which Viola adopts for herself), Stephen Orgel's 1996 *Impersonations* 'is a book about what has been unnoticeable and invisible'. Orgel's arguments always relate back to the ways in which the fact of Shakespeare's boy actors affected the Renaissance reception of gender and sexuality in performance. Paul Hammond's *Figuring Sex Between Men from Shakespeare to Rochester* (2002) looks at the homoerotic additions and subtractions that Shakespeare makes to one of his source texts, *Gl'Ingannati*:

> the idea that a man might with equal enthusiasm bed a pretty boy or a pretty girl does surface in *Twelfth Night*. . . . Shakespeare imagines characters puzzled by their feelings, rather at sea emotionally, and finding that their sense of self is bound up with their love for an unreadable and unattainable other. (Hammond, *Figuring Sex*, p. 96)

Hammond goes on to give a careful description of what he sees as a latent and linguistically anchored homosexual relationship between

Sebastian and Antonio. Stanley Wells explores this same relationship through choices made in modern productions, in his *Looking for Sex in Shakespeare* (2004). Live theatre, like gay literary interpretations, can make textually silent loves dare to speak their name.

Finally, a return to 1985, and Barbara Everett's article 'Or What You Will', a fitting conclusion to this chapter. Everett is sensitively alive to *Twelfth Night*'s comedy and desire as she seeks to describe its shifts and balances of tone, its elusive and curious atmosphere. She achieves a moment of crescendo in twentieth-century criticism when she maps the play's various pathways of desire thus:

> Uncomplicated though the plot is, when the twins come together there also come together what one might list as Orsino's love for Olivia, Olivia's for Cesario, Olivia's for Sebastian, Olivia's for Viola, Viola's for Orsino, Orsino's for Cesario, Orsino's for Viola, Sebastian's for Viola, Sebastian's for Antonio, Antonio's for Sebastian, Antonio's for Cesario, Antonio's for Viola.   (White, *New Casebooks*, p. 210)

She misses Viola's for Olivia and Cesario's for Orsino. But whatever one wills, and however hard, one can't have it all ways.

6 Commentary: The Play in Performance

ACT I

Act I, scene i

0.1 Our first impressions include a world of music. We see an important man enter with his personal attendant and others of a high social status. Shakespeare's original audience would have known this immediately through their costuming. Perhaps the man is distant from the rest of the court and is distinct from them in the way he is dressed. If the music is being performed by a musician or musicians on stage then it may be brought on as part of the court, or the man may encounter it as an already established on-stage presence. These opening moments could help to establish a recognizable social world of easily discernible hierarchies, or something more fantastic, fairy-tale-like, or abstract in the stage design. The setting could be inside or out of doors, in a lavish interior, or a garden signifying any time of the year, or the world could be more suggestive of austerity and absence (which would make the language itself work harder).

1–7 This is justly one of the most famous openings of all Shakespeare's plays. It introduces us to a self-consciously conditional and beguiling world of sensuous languor and longing. These lines will begin to establish the kind of masculinity the actor wants to portray and to show how this relates to the man's expressions of desire. The man wants music. This seems to have stopped before he speaks because he asks for it to 'play on'. The actor could take as long as he chooses before asking for 'excess of it'; meanwhile the audience may begin to notice how romantic he is. Is he standing or moving around, sitting or lying down? Is he speaking to himself, the audience, or to those around him? The court may actively encourage his musings, or may appear tired of them. One or more of them may be portrayed as having a special care over the man, perhaps bringing him food or drink, or nurturing him physically. After all, his words express both hunger and desire. How far are we looking at an exclusively male environment? Some or all of the attendants may be female.

Shakespeare is brave enough to allow our first impressions of his language to be underscored. Music, even if it sounds languorous, suggests creative vitality and effort but how far does the choice of melody complement the poetry? Do we hear the music encouraging the man's words, or perhaps competing with what he is trying to articulate? The music may help to illustrate the man's aesthetic taste and emotions. So, the audience encounters a sensually demanding moment of verbal and non-verbal sounds and, in deciding for ourselves whether or not the music we hear really *is* the 'food of love', we establish an automatic relationship with the central figure of the moment.

Certainly, the man appears to be metaphorically feeding, or at least trying to. His words signify an artistic as well as a sexual encounter. Hunger and greed, the desire for 'excess', are easily associated with lust, a sexual appetite which 'dies' with a self-consuming orgasm. The music itself has 'a dying fall' (line 4), strains which the man sees as representative of physical surges of desire. Sound also transmutes into smell for him as he imagines 'a bank of violets' which, with the breeze rippling through them, inhale and lose their scent at one and the same time (lines 6–7). Here the argument develops to a further awareness of the transitory, and the man asks for the music to stop. Perhaps it has become disconnected with what he is trying to realize for himself. The musicians may even leave.

8–15   Now he speaks without music. The contrast could achieve a greater openness, possibly a vulnerability, and restore a sense of balance. He has moved on. His appetite is satisfied; his taste for things sweet has been blunted. Now he begins an abstract musing on the 'spirit of love' (line 8). Just how far he has been talking to himself until this point, rather than to those around him, may now become clear, or he may be seen to become even more introverted and disconnected from the established social context. For him, love is almost too vast and impossible to comprehend. As broad and as absorbing as the ocean, it overwhelms things great and small in no time at all. If a naturalistic setting has been created visually, there may even be the sound of waves breaking. If the man is exasperated with his thoughts, the tone may move to the self-consciously humorous; if he is trying to deliver an essay, then we may begin to sense the absurdity of his plight and wonder how genuine it is supposed to be. He eventually arrives at 'fancy' (imagination as well as sexual attraction) and 'fantastical' (intensely imaginative, possibly surreal), which seem to be as true for himself as for the ideas he has been contemplating.

16–22 Curio interrupts out of boredom or sympathy, and splinters the verse line into three parts. His is the first name we learn and it suggests curiosity or even a cure for love. He puns on 'hart', which the man, still utterly self-absorbed, hears as 'heart' and relates to the object of his desires: Olivia. The first time we hear the name it trips off his tongue as part of a regular verse line. The name is immediately associated with life-giving qualities and cleansing (lines 18–19). Yet, the man then turns the pun against himself, identifying with the hunted 'hart', rather than the hunter. Once again, he is becoming introverted and solipsistic (lines 20–2). Another interruption comes with the entrance of a new attendant who changes the direction of his verse on the half-line (line 22). The entrance could involve a change in the on-stage grouping.

23–31 The messenger of love (anonymous for audiences, significantly named Valentine for readers) brings disappointment, and paints for us a stage picture of Olivia. The language is gentle and pious. She will mourn and meditate, nun-like and veiled, for seven years over her brother's death (lines 25–31). This thumbnail sketch may conjure up the man's counterpart, someone else who is apparently caught up in her own inner world. The 'brine' of Olivia's tears associates her with the man's own hungry ocean of love (line 11); both are suggestive of longing and regret.

32–40   The man is changed by the news, interpreting Olivia's mourning as a prelude to the love she may show to himself. He also plays down the depth of love possible between brother and sister. Love moves through his speech again as an abstract ideal, the incidentally phallic resonance of Cupid's 'rich golden shaft' (line 34) bringing the act of sex again to the fore. And his extraordinary anatomization of Olivia breaks the verse line itself up into rich vowel sounds, with a curious, centrally echoic music: 'That live in her, when liver, brain, and heart', the last word of the line taking us back to the notion of someone desiring whilst another is being hunted. This yet to be named man now crowns himself 'one self king' over Olivia's passion, judgement and sentiment (represented by liver, brain, and heart), self-promoted by his desires and imaginings.

His final rhyming couplet expresses his will to escape 'to sweet beds of flowers' rather than to win Olivia. The last line automatically slows down the actor's voice with its monosyllabic range of hard consonant sounds in its first half ('Love-thoughts lie rich when'), tripping vowel sounds ('canopied') and gentler consonants as the rhyme is achieved ('flowers'). The phrase 'thoughts lie rich' may arrest us with its pun on 'lie', especially in the wake of the man's own 'rich' thoughts. How quickly he escapes (or will escape) into further paralytic musings will reflect his mood, as will the reactions of those around him.

Act I, scene ii

0.1   In a present-day production a shipwreck may be staged at this point, showing the crew being cruelly separated. In powerful contrast to the waves we might have heard in the first scene, here we encounter the ocean wreaking havoc. Much of this could be expressed through the use of sound and stage-lighting. But there is calm after the storm. A young woman enters the stage with a sea captain and other sailor survivors. She is of a higher social status than her companions. The mood may be one of fear, bewilderment, exhaustion, thankfulness.

1–4   The young woman speaks first. Her question betrays a sense of confusion as she tries to re-establish control and order. It is only a half-line, perhaps indicative of breathlessness or nervous excitement. By addressing them as 'friends' she creates an immediate sense of camaraderie. Perhaps the Captain is already seen nurturing his passenger–mistress. His reply names the entire stage space as the country: Illyria (modern-day Croatia), and could be delivered with a variety of inflections: gratitude, warning, suspicion, magic, or be plainly informative. Her reply is almost desperate, but it is also her first full line of verse. Suddenly she reveals her brother's death. The music in these lines makes their poignancy even greater. The openness of 'Illyria' is balanced with the closed, doubtful, humming quality of 'Elysium', the classical abode of the dead. This light linguistic touch comes just as the young woman is finding a way to restore her own sense of equilibrium. We may already connect her loss of a brother with Olivia's (I.i.25–31) and it contributes another similar thread to the dramatic texture. But is he *really* dead? She appeals to the sailors.

5–16   The Captain replies for them. On learning that she is lucky to be alive, the young woman moves quickly from shock and regret to hope, within the same line (line 6). The Captain reflects her hope back to her in a richly embroidered account aimed to comfort (lines 7–16). This tale from a seasoned sea-farer gives us our first impressions of the brother. He is strong, with the keen edge of a survivor, binding himself to a mast and surfing across the waves like Arion (a musician of Greek legend who escaped being murdered at sea).

17–38   The young woman gives the Captain money in return for his encouragement and we hear another name: Orsino, a name repeated, like that of Illyria itself, by the young woman (lines 24–5). The name is suggestive of something bear-like (a man perhaps madly bated), and of the constellations Ursa Major and Ursa Minor: the Pole Star by which sailors navigate. The audience may wonder whether or not such a name suits the man we have just met. The young woman also associates his name with her own father, and remembers that Orsino was spoken of as a bachelor. The world outside the scope of the essential dramatic narrative is important to *Twelfth Night*, and often represents the longing and regrets of its characters, as it may do here. The affection that Orsino has for Olivia is here reiterated by the Captain, making it clear that it was Duke Orsino we encountered in the opening scene.

38–61 Loss of a beloved brother is here the rich parallel between two female characters. The young woman's empathy for Olivia is palpably expressed; she longs to serve her, perhaps hoping thereby to conceal her own anxiety and to defer her discovery. The young woman really knows that she has no choice other than to trust the Captain. She calls him 'thee', but her speech (lines 44–6) shows how little she knows him. The Captain's verse half-line may suggest a pause before the young woman replies. Trusting in the kindness of strangers, and showing familiar respect to them, has to be one of her main strategies for survival in this foreign land. Her promise to pay him 'bounteously' is to inspire further help on his part.

She may start disguising herself right away, possibly with some items rescued from the shipwreck. A production may be able to establish these as being some of her brother's clothes. Shakespeare's original audience might have laughed at 'eunuch': the boy actor's voice would not yet have broken. Perhaps this prompts a comparison with Orsino's masculinity. The young woman promises music and singing, which we know Orsino will associate with his own desire and longing (lines 54–6). She is a performer. The Captain promises to remain silent, like a mute. Depending on how and when she starts to disguise herself, the young woman's femininity may begin to disappear by the end of the scene. She closes the scene as she started it, on a half-line, but is now journeying with certainty forwards, and establishing her new voice and sense of direction. The Captain's rhyming couplet should have finished the scene, but she herself takes control at the end, jauntily pushing beyond his rhyme, and deciding on the next step.

This scene presents the discovery of new worlds, new information, and new possibilities. A young woman decides on new and brave solutions, and shares her expedient need to live creatively. Her self-consciously fictional framework is fragile and relies on the strength of her disguise.

Act I, scene iii

0.1   Now we encounter rotund exuberance, a disarming contrast to romantic musings and survival narratives. We have moved from shipwreck to physical wreck and meet two new characters: a slobbish, boorish, but noble drunk, and a lady-in-waiting. The audience could learn a lot about their relationship by the way they enter. Does the lady-in-waiting seem affectionately tolerant of the drunk nobleman, for example? What are their respective ages? A difference in age could have great bearing on their relationship and how it may develop. If the woman offers nurture, then this may seem maternal, but it may also be (mis)interpreted as flirtatious, or perhaps there is a definite erotic connection between them?

1–2   We have entered the soundscape of prose (which makes up two-thirds of this play). Here is unbuttoning and relaxation. Like the young woman we've just met, the drunkard starts the scene off with a question, and one which acts as a contradiction to the passionate empathy for Olivia we have just witnessed. The tone, mood and music of the drama have again changed completely. His drunk and questioning expostulation may be spoken moderately to himself, to his companion, or directly to the audience. The latter choice would immediately instigate the noble drunkard's persistent, comic ingratiation, the appeal of which may become crucial to the overall dramatic texture. He pauses to reflect. His own answer carries with it the potential for self-pity. Depending on the length and quality of the pause after the question, his answer could get a laugh. We have already met two major characters for whom 'care is an enemy to life', and here our suspicions are borne out about a third: Olivia. But this drunkard seems not to care at all.

3–6   We learn his first name and status, and have confirmation that this is part of his usual behaviour. We also learn where we are. Sir Toby is Olivia's cousin, a guest in her house, and his drunken behaviour is a source of on-going irritation. Her reiteration of the relationship could suggest that she is speaking slowly in the face of his drunken gaze. In her apparently mild admonishment, Maria may also share affectionately some of Sir Toby's warmth and humour. We do not know the time of day, but the further into the morning it is, the more outrageous Sir Toby's behaviour. Or, we may be in the small hours with the dialogue being spoken with an urgency so as not to disturb the rest of the house. We could be inside or out of doors. Either way, we may make our first impressions of Olivia's home, which we may compare with Orsino's. Sir Toby's reply in the form of a legal pun (line 6) could sound like a drunken play on words.

7–15 'Confine', offered as part of a helpful suggestion, is taken by Sir Toby as a threat. His reply of incredulity is given in wonderfully elastic prose, aided by the sound of fricatives: 'confine myself no finer', humorously stretching out his sense of eager dismissal. It could lead to a visual joke about his physical size, perhaps even a physical advance on the lady-in-waiting. The rest of his reply shows an admirable nonchalance about the importance of clothes – clothes disorderly and spoilt, perhaps dirty with his night's drinking. Does his costume contrast with Maria's: his perhaps garish and carefree, hers more sober?

Warnings about Sir Toby being undone by drink seem like too little, too late, but could help to register the lady-in-waiting's degree of interest in him. Again, she appeals to her mistress as an authority, fleshing out further our expectations of Olivia as someone who may be a little interfering and, for Sir Toby, apt to be censorious. In her reply to Sir Toby, the lady-in-waiting's prose becomes teasingly elastic. The senses of 'knight' and 'night' could easily become transposed when heard.

16–22 Sir Andrew Aguecheek is prominently named as Sir Toby's choice of wooer for Olivia. Sir Toby's description may generate laughter, especially if there is a slight pause before either 'tall' or 'man', but its obvious irrelevance, especially when said quickly ('tall' could mean courageous), can be enjoyed just the same. And then the truth becomes clear. Sir Andrew is seriously wealthy, and herein lies Sir Toby's interest (line 20). For Maria he is an imprudent spendthrift who can easily spend all his ducats in one year.

23–40 The actor waiting in the wings probably hears what is said about him just before he enters. What we learn promises further musical and linguistic exuberance. The lady-in-waiting produces eloquent contradiction, her prose sliding gracefully through 'quarreller', 'quarrelling' and 'quickly', from 'the gift of a coward' to 'the gift of a grave' (lines 27–30). The conflict between her perceptions and Sir Toby's comic defensiveness propels the dialogue forward and beyond her punning accusation that Sir Toby and Sir Andrew are drunk 'nightly'.

Sir Toby turns the direction at the beginning of line 35, with his tribute to Olivia (humorous because it could be affectionate, but cynical as well as mock-heroic). He changes direction further in his affectionate appeal to the lady-in-waiting: 'What, wench!', very likely the kind of attention she has been craving. And then something fantastical, an obscure classical allusion heralds the first appearance of 'Agueface'. This nickname emphasizes the physical contrast between this pair of comedians and reminds us that Shakespeare was writing for a particular company of actors, embracing their visual potential for comedy as he did so.

40–1 How fantastical is Sir Andrew? How, for instance, does his costume contrast with that of Sir Toby? He is wealthy, so perhaps his clothes are much finer. He may well be very lean and sickly looking, possibly neurotic, but he is still on the look out for revels. How old is he: over-the-hill, or more of the young dandy? Either way he may be beguilingly naive, and the audience may fall for him at first sight.

41–56 Sir Andrew could enter with a child-like enthusiasm, otherwise why use his companion's full name if he is only feet away? Or, perhaps, Sir Andrew enters genuinely looking for Sir Toby? At last we learn Sir Toby's surname, which, like Sir Andrew's, refers to a physical characteristic: Belch, and it's repeated for us. How far does the audience already suspect, from what has been said, that any affection on Sir Andrew's part is sorely misplaced? How do they greet? With a warm hug? If Sir Toby has been resting drunk on the floor, perhaps he may even struggle to arise. He may even kiss Sir Andrew heartily and humorously on the lips, causing a ripple of laughter, or even a look of disgust, in front of the lady-in-waiting. Sir Andrew's short greeting to her has a crisp but gauche internal rhyme ('you' and 'shrew', line 43), which indicates his buffoonery, but 'shrew' is also his attempt at flirtation. This breaks into some quick repartee and an extended misunderstanding about the name of Olivia's servant. Her name, we learn, is Mary, and Sir Andrew's slowness to grasp this indicates his tendency towards the clottish. He does not seem to be easily embarrassed; Sir Toby is probably enjoying every minute of it. Sir Toby's advice, humour breaking through a mixture of kindness and patronizing control (lines 52–3), may be spoken as an aside, but could be funnier if Mary heard every word. Sir Andrew's reference to 'this company' may allude to the audience, and could help to establish a privileged relationship between them and the actor. Mary moves to leave; she's had enough.

57–75   Sir Andrew repeats Sir Toby's words without any apparent filtering of thought (lines 57–60). Sir Andrew may even imitate Sir Toby's voice and physical gesture. Humorous this may be, but it also illustrates Sir Toby's control. Mary reacts with either confusion or mild disdain, prompting further dialogue. 'Hand' may be sexually pointed with innuendo, especially if Mary pauses before she says it. Sir Andrew's response may further the sexual metaphor (lines 63–4), but his attempt at self-irony falls awkwardly (lines 63–4), and Mary mocks him further by being contentiously flirtatious (line 65). The joke is that Sir Andrew probably assumes he's making good progress but, once Mary starts inviting him (possibly) to feel her breasts (lines 65–6), nothing could be further from the truth.

Sir Andrew now sees the way open for him to start calling her 'sweetheart'. Again he misinterprets her saying 'it's dry' as referring to his hand (perhaps indicative of further physical contact), rather than to her own wit. She is in complete control of the situation: her crisp, witty answers contrasting with his longer open musings and questions (lines 68–74). She has jests at her fingers' ends, and Sir Andrew is wrapped around her little finger. She leaves the stage triumphantly and celebrating the full possession of her own sexuality with her retort, 'Marry, now I let go your hand I am *barren* [my italics]'.

76–84   Sir Toby speaks for the first time in almost twenty lines, possibly intervening to offer his friend a drink, or longing that they both had some with them. He is critical and comforting at the same time. Sir Andrew has been 'put down' terribly, and Sir Toby is not going to let him forget it. Sir Andrew's reply shows a likeable, though potentially irritating optimism on his part, drawing together Sir Toby's offer of wine to recollect occasions when he's been drunk. He seems to be making the best of his embarrassment. He's like a child who picks himself up again after a fall, and runs on.

Sir Andrew's self-deprecating humour continues. Lines 79–80 would have offended the Puritans of Shakespeare's day, and lines 81–2 may get a knowing laugh in English productions since 1996 because of the outbreak of mad cow disease. Sir Andrew is unstoppable and, confirming Mary's opinion of him as 'a great quarreller' (line 27), he jumps on the smallest interjection of Sir Toby's with a suitable riposte (line 84).

84–104   With Sir Andrew's declaration to leave we may glimpse his sense of failure. Sir Toby captures his attention again with the sudden use of French. Not of great subtlety in mind, Sir Andrew is again at a loss (line 87), but moves on to become wistful (lines 89–90). The wit in the following exchange relies on the visual joke of Sir Andrew's hair, often a lank, floppy blonde wig in productions. It won't curl by nature, but he could have learned to curl it artificially (with a pun on 'tongues' for 'tongs'). There is a moment of misplaced vanity when Sir Andrew calls attention to his hair, in search of admiration (line 95). And then comes a bawdy joke, which may well inspire some sort of suggestive re-enactment (lines 96–8). Sir Toby imagines the desire of Sir Andrew's future wife, having such good sex with him that she will either pull out his hair with erotic excitement, or have her fingers continually running through it (lines 96–8).

Sir Andrew's repeating his intention of leaving (lines 84–5 and 99), in response to this sexual vision, signifies either an immature fear of sex, or perhaps a fragile masculinity. His excuses remind us that the Countess Olivia will not be seen, and that the Count Orsino is trying to woo her in any case (lines 100–1). Sir Toby's verbal encouragement may be emphasized with some other friendly gestures (lines 102–4) because Sir Andrew decides to stay for another month. Perhaps Sir Toby embraces his companion on 'Tut, there's life in't, man.'

105–32   Suddenly, Sir Andrew is back on course, quixotic and capricious, delighting 'in masques and revels sometimes altogether'. He's ready for sport and utters a nonsensical boast. Sir Toby steers the dialogue towards further considerations of trifles as light as air and only of the moment (line 108). Sir Andrew puts into circulation the proverb 'cutting a caper against care' (line 113) – if in doubt, dance and forget your worries – and explicitly associates dancing with sex: 'back-trick' (with echoes of bed-trick). Perhaps this discussion of dancing is accompanied by comic examples of the forms referred to: (galliard, caper, back-trick, coranto, jig, cinquepace).

Sir Toby continues the mutual boasting. The identity of Mistress Mall is far less important than the idea that she is sexually attractive and should not have to be covered up by a curtain. There is a whiff of toilet humour, punning on the French 'cinque' and 'sink' (lines 121–2), before Sir Toby focuses on their abundantly innate talents through reference to the heavens themselves, playing on 'constitu-tion' for 'constellation' (lines 124–5 and 128–9). Sir Andrew brings us back down to earth by referring to his socks (whether dun, damned, flame, lemon, or divers-coloured, see Chapter 1). Bullish and bois-terous behaviour is suggested again with Sir Toby's reference to Taurus. Sir Andrew's dance could be as long lasting and as comic as a production decides. We may see Sir Andrew clumsily lifting up, or kicking, his long legs, prompting Sir Toby's own on-stage enjoy-ment and laughter, and even encouraging a round of applause from the audience.

Act I, scene iv

0.1   Orsino's messenger enters, so we are back with his court in a non-specified location. Here is the shipwrecked young woman in her eunuch's disguise. How recognizable is she? Her movements might have changed, and she may appear nervous or uncomfortable.

1–8   The young woman's plan and disguise seem to be working. After just three days, she is settling into Orsino's household (his status is reiterated by his servant, line 1), and has clearly caught her master's attention, with whom she seems to have become noticeably familiar. Our young woman has called herself Cesario. We have here our first impressions of how she speaks as a eunuch. Her voice will not be deep, but we may notice some difference in its timbre, a timbre which the actor will have to sustain for as long as the disguise continues. Cesario gives a spirited reply, a slight rebuff, and may appear quite confident. Her question about Orsino's constancy (possibly there is a slight pause on her part before she asks about it) may provide our first sense of the growing attraction she has for him (lines 6–7). Her colleague's brief reply may suggest that he is taken aback by Cesario's mild rebuttal. Or, he may simply be interrupted by the entrance of Orsino.

8.1–12   Orsino enters. Do we detect any change in him? Does he, for example, seem more business-like and decisive? He is attended by Curio and probably some of the same lords whom we saw at the beginning. In fact, the entrance itself may appear to be almost identical, harking back to that enigmatic opening. He does not see Cesario immediately, suggesting that she and the other servant are obscured in a different part of the stage; they may simply be more up-stage than Orsino, and on the same side as his entrance. Orsino is direct and has a single purpose: to see his eunuch. 'Cesario, ho?' could sound casually affectionate. Cesario comes forward, possibly causing some of the attendants to shift their positions, and so allowing the audience to see how they react to the arrival of the Duke's new favourite. Orsino's command for them all to stand 'aloof' could, depending on how secret he wants to be, clear the stage of other attendants completely, or they may move further away and be able to overhear the ensuing dialogue between their master and his new servant.

12–29   Orsino instigates the manoeuvre back into verse, the form
most suitable for discussing his romantic feelings and, here, having a
heightened degree of intimacy, not least in the sudden closeness of
relationship suggested between Orsino and Cesario. He adopts 'thee'
as his chosen diction, contrasting with the 'you' used between
Cesario and the other servant. The word 'unclasped' slows down the
end of line 13, and could be more than faintly suggestive of Orsino's
desirous intent. The word may summon up the removal of clothing
as a visual image. This could richly suggest an intensity in Orsino's
urging, which may begin to raise questions about the nature of his
intimacy with Cesario. Do we see Cesario as a woman being fasci-
nated enough to return Orsino's gaze, or do we see Cesario shying
away from encouraging him too much? The image of Cesario standing at Olivia's doors, rooted to the spot (line 17), harks forward to
a future episode, and we may perceive Cesario already seeming
challenged by it.

There is an eagerness on Cesario's part, as we hear her finishing
Orsino's half-lines of verse (line 18), reciprocated by Orsino's similar
manoeuvre (line 29). Orsino gives Cesario carte-blanche to do whatever is necessary to win over Olivia for him (line 21). An anticipatory
tension between Orsino's ideas and passions and Cesario's doubts
that Olivia will be moved by them is carefully established. Cesario is
beginning her role as go-between. Orsino's describing himself as a
'nuncio' (messenger) chimes as quaintly archaic, even self-mocking.
Calling Cesario 'lad' reiterates the careful contrasts that ripple
through this short scene, and may even be suggestive of parental
affection.

30–4   Orsino playfully deconstructs Cesario's appearance of
masculinity. From another man, as it were, this could suggest a subtly
aggressive desire to control. Diana is evoked in relation to the
smooth whiteness of Cesario's moon-like face. Manhood was known
in this period partly by the appearance of a beard, not impossible for
a boy actor, but certainly so for Cesario, and a eunuch would not be
able to grow one. The irony is that Orsino sounds as if he is seeing
through Cesario's disguise (lines 32–4), and he may even do so. This
would make for a conservative, hetero-normative interpretation:

Orsino knows that Cesario is a woman all along, but pretends not to (for whatever reason), or perhaps he simply wishes Cesario were a woman. A more complex choice would be to explore why Orsino is making such observations about another male, and what our reactions are (and why) when we see and hear him do this. Is Orsino being subliminally flirtatious? There could be physical contact between the two at this point: playful, seductive, perhaps even verging on the slightly menacing. Does Cesario adjust her physical gait, suddenly exaggerate her masculinity, in an attempt to strengthen her disguise in response to Orsino's strange advances and comments? Or does she permit them?

35–42   Orsino changes direction. He checks himself. He excuses his observations through admiring the appropriateness of Cesario's physical appearance instead. And then he makes sure that the moment returns to the public sphere by calling for a large number of attendants (line 36). By so doing he is continuing to lavish attention on Cesario, but balances it with his sudden declaration that he wants to be alone (lines 37–8). He makes an absurd and rash promise (lines 38–40), the extravagance and impact of which could inspire a laugh, depending on how it is contextualized. Cesario manages to make a quick reply, though she has, modestly and perhaps awkwardly, remained passive and silent for ten lines. The tension established in this scene is permitted a brief burst of relief in Cesario's final rhyming couplet, chiming 'strife' and 'wife'. Is this muttered to herself, or spoken pleadingly to the audience? If the attendant actors have already started waiting on Cesario, then this may determine how the assembled company leaves the stage. Orsino could leave first, spurred by his impetuosity (perhaps echoing the end of Act I, scene i), or he may remain dolefully on stage, and exit last.

Act I, scene v

1–17   We could be outside or indoors for this scene, possibly the same setting as for Act I, scene iii. It is time to complicate both the narrative and the verbal texture. A Clown is introduced; he may be recognizable by his costume. He does not reply to Mary's question about where he has been, suggesting an enigmatic immediacy about him. Her concern could be genuine and hint at a long-established, affectionate relationship, or she may simply be behaving archly towards a social inferior. Mary is a lady-in-waiting, a gentlewoman, though she could be portrayed as more of a maid servant. This would make her social status lower than Sir Toby's, but higher than the Clown's. She starts off by using 'thee' as the familiar verbal register (lines 1 and 8). The Clown's subjunctive utterances, couched (until line 24) in the third person, seem to require a more critical distancing on her part, and she starts to use 'you' (line 11). He refers to her in the familiar second person 'thy' for the first time (line 24). The Clown is in complete control of the dramatic texture of this opening dialogue, the rudder for its direction. Mary's reiteration that he will be hanged for his absence, or thrown out, may reflect his social status. If not dressed in traditional motley (a variously coloured uniform to indicate his status as a fool), the production may find another way of presenting him as an outsider. His costume may suggest, for example, a tramp, bohemian, or traveller. Mary's reference to the wars (line 11) may be spoken with reproof or regret and could lead to the Clown being depicted more like a soldier of fortune.

18–28   His verbal dexterity provides a constant buzz of comic energy, propelling the action forward like a well-oiled machine. His crude sexual joke (about the length of an imaginary husband's penis, line 18) is an early example of this quality of verbal exchange. Mary breaks briefly into foolery herself and we catch something of her earlier wit in her pun on argumentative 'points', and the 'points' which attached the doublet to the hose (lines 22–3). The Clown suddenly turns serious, mentioning Eve and making explicit reference to Mary's relationship with Sir Toby, retrospectively providing a context for his sexual talk about 'bad marriage' a few lines before. *Why* is he saying what he does? If the Clown is revelling in gossip then he could really be enjoying himself, or he may be more cynical and detached? He is silenced by Mary, either playfully or seriously (possibly implying the physical interaction of a slight cuff), and by the entrance of Olivia.

28.1   What are our first impressions of Olivia? We have heard much about her. How old is she? She is dressed in mourning, is probably veiled, and seems settled in silence. Feste is comfortable enough or bold enough to speak first.

29–33   The Clown may be talking to himself, to the fool's head on his jester's stick, to Mary, or to one of the attendants. He may speak out to the audience, establishing a relationship with us, and drawing us further in to his comic perspective. He seems to be mocking pedantry. It may help a modern audience for him to pronounce 'Quinapalus' as 'Qui n'a pas lu' (Who has not read).

34–67   Olivia appears immediately confrontational. The Clown reflects this back to her. Her word 'dry' to describe his kind of comedy recalls Mary's use of the word to Sir Andrew (I.iii.69–72). Her charge of unreliability ('dishonest') may suggest some anger on her part. She finds the Clown irritating. Perhaps we see her only just being able to endure his torrent of prose (lines 38–48). Are her attendants more amused than she is? She may gesture for them to take the Clown before she actually asks them to, in which case he may be backing away during his speech and pushing his luck.

The Clown's wit here is one of obsessive logic, dismissing Olivia's 'dry' and 'dishonest', and escaping into his own space of verbal control. And somehow Olivia's initial guard is falling. Perhaps his talk of transgressing virtue and patched up sin arrests her, to question afresh her absolutist position of prolonged mourning. Continuous grief will neither make her a better person, nor make greater her dead brother's virtues. She reiterates her resistance (line 49), but the Clown's reply (lines 50–3) encourages her at last to engage with him, possibly out of toleration and habit.

The Clown's catechism (lines 57–67, for which the pair could adopt different positions) supplies a mock-religious context and makes more comic his affectionate use of 'madonna' (my lady). She may give in nonchalantly (lines 59–60), if not graciously. Her reply to the suggestion that her brother's soul is in hell could be petulant or even angry. She's fallen for the Clown's joke, and we may even see the pair of them share a laugh together when the Clown makes his conclusion (line 65–7). It may seem in poor taste, but it could make Olivia momentarily step out of her mourning. Here is an opportunity for her to show real affection for the Clown.

68–93   Olivia turns to one of her servants, Malvolio. He may literally step forward into our attention as her chief attendant. He has remained silent for thirty-nine lines. Have we noticed what he's been doing during this time: sneering, ignoring, or (what would be the most sympathetic portrayal) trying not to enjoy the Clown too much? Olivia names him for the audience, who may laugh to consider how far he appears to be like his name: Malvolio ('I wish illwill'). If he is played old, then he may appear to be crabbed and hopelessly set in his mean little ways, if young then his hopeless pride, aloofness, and detachment may be more apparent. We see him being unable to concede to any change of tone, least of all one involving levity.

His mean-spirited reply (lines 70–2) may suggest his jealousy that Olivia should have spent so long lavishing her attention on the Clown. Malvolio evades the Clown's quick-spirited rebuff, and ignores Olivia's invitation to answer it. Instead he delivers a gratuitous insult (lines 78–84). The Clown, he says, has suffered put-downs by those of apparently less wit, and his ability to be comic relies too much on others' encouragement and attention.

Olivia arbitrates between the two of them (lines 85–91) and herself delivers a public put-down to Malvolio, accusing him of 'self-love'. She seems quick to come to the protection and defence of her Clown, and this may be a moment of real tenderness on her part. A useful Shakespearian parallel to bear in mind is the relationship between the Countess of Roussillon and her fool, Lavatch, in *All's Well That Ends Well*. The licensing of a similar kind of clowning in both Roussillon and Illyria seems long established, a fact the Clown celebrates (lines 92–3).

94–104   And now the audience can feel satisfied that the various narratives are beginning to become intertwined. We know that this 'well attended' 'fair young man' (lines 97–8) is Cesario and, having already met Sir Toby, we can imagine the off-stage reality of their encounter. Here, we may have some empathy with Olivia's reaction (lines 101–2). If we are sensitive to the play's alternative title, *What You Will*, then we have Olivia suddenly becoming metatheatrically associated with it (lines 103–4), with a meaning suggestive of extemporariness and urgency.

105–9 This is a moment of almost private exchange between Olivia and her Clown (some attendants may still be on stage). The Clown could go and sit at her feet. Olivia is attempting to smooth the conflict between the Clown and Malvolio a few lines earlier. She calls him 'sir'; she is respectful. His fooling is 'old' (tired), which may be suggestive of the Clown's age and a long established relationship between the two of them. He recognizes her concern, but his words change direction as he talks about the approach of Sir Toby.

110–32 Does Olivia betray a slight sense in which she, too, is amused by Sir Toby's inimitable slovenliness and inappropriate timing? Sir Toby probably belches or farts – a reason for his cursing the pickled herring (lines 115–16). The more restrained his noise and drunkenness, the greater the humour may be. There is a moment of spontaneous affection from Sir Toby to the Clown (line 116), which Olivia interrupts. Sir Toby mishears 'lethargy' as 'lechery', and ostentatiously protests about one of his greatest vices. Sir Toby's line before his exit is a further example of his will not to be contained or restricted, but to pursue his own inclinations without compromise. Olivia has a further exchange with her Clown, who in his verbal support may also seem to take on the role of counsellor and comforter. She knows she can speak easily to him, and slips into a direct and searching diction (line 124). The Clown's exit (line 131) is not marked in the Folio and he could remain silently on stage.

133–57 Despite Malvolio's pride, pedantry and self-satisfied censures, something that he says persuades Olivia that she should see Cesario. The short sharp questioning on Olivia's part (lines 144–9) may bear comparison with the way we have just heard her speak to the Clown; Malvolio's replies (lines 145–55) may suggest that he is trying to compete with the Clown's wit for his Lady's attention. In the end, it is Malvolio's description of Cesario's youth, his way of speaking 'shrewishly' (with bite and petulance), which persuades Olivia that he is worth meeting. Perhaps she senses the opportunity for further mocking and clowning, especially if her Clown has remained on stage.

158–60   There is just time for Olivia to put on her veil (potentially her own mask of revelry, as well as protection) before Cesario enters. We may see Mary veiling herself too, which would account for Cesario's uncertainty as she enters. Cesario's mistake may arise out of naivety, or nerves, but could also serve to emphasize the high social status of Mary.

161–77   Olivia begins playfully, self-protectively. Cesario breaks off from the start of her formal address to question the purpose of her performance. Her first speech is made self-consciously and could reveal something of Cesario's own character: something which, subliminally, Olivia may register and begin to find attractive (lines 162–8). There seems to be honest self-deprecation, too, when Cesario reveals that she is sensitive to even the smallest rebuttal (lines 167–8). Olivia seems to be both disarmed and charmed. Her first question is matter of fact (line 169), her second (line 174) could be incredulous, mildly scornful, or we may perceive the first glimmers of flirtation. Olivia may turn to appeal to, or involve, her own Clown at this point. Cesario's words 'I am not that I play' are gnomic, almost riddle-like, and, if taken literally, could prompt Olivia to see beyond her disguise. Perhaps she does.

178–210   By now, thirteen lines too late, Cesario's prepared speech has been contextualized as something rehearsed and insincere, contrasting with her own open, easy and bumbling reactions. Mary may perceive a hint in Olivia's excuses (lines 188–93), or there may be a glance between them, because she invites Cesario to leave. Her spirited refusal and persistence bring us back to the purpose of her visit (lines 196–7). There are a few lines of successful persuasion on Cesario's part. Olivia's persistent tendency to catechize (lines 203–4, like the Clown) does not serve to provide the critical distance and control she is seeking. After Cesario's reply, couched with reference to the secrecy and divinity of virginity (possibly a slippage from her male language, lines 206–8), Olivia is making sure that she is alone with him. The scene shifts from the securely public to the vulnerably intimate as Mary, the Clown (if he's still on stage) and the other attendants leave.

211–27   The dialogue takes a definitely flirtatious turn with reference to Orsino's bosom and heart and, as if encouraged by the thought of this, Cesario asks to see Olivia's face. Why? Mutual feminine curiosity to see her competition for Orsino, or for less easily definable, more subjectively erotic reasons? Olivia's exaggerated self-comparison with a picture (perhaps recalling Sir Toby's reference to Mistress Mall, I.iii.119) can often inspire encouraging laughter in the audience, and sets up Cesario's bold quip about the nature of true beauty. The tone of the scene changes when Olivia reveals her face; the energy becomes more intimate and intense.

228–38   Cesario dares to break into verse. She may pause before doing so; we may hear the difference. She is a social inferior, and the contrast of the change is marked, because we have heard prose for virtually the whole of this scene until now. To Olivia's ears, it may sound as though this messenger has changed gear. She must keep up with him, but at the same time it requires vulnerability on her part to do so. For a few lines yet, Olivia remains resolutely in prose. Her extraordinary self-anatomization, framing her beauty as a bequest (what she wills), makes death a part of the immediate dramatic texture. We may recollect Orsino's earlier anatomization of Olivia as well (I.i.36–8). Cesario's first five lines of verse here bear interesting comparison to the first seventeen of Shakespeare's Sonnets (especially Sonnets 1, 3, 9 and 11). 'Copy' has now become a metaphor for physical procreation, in contrast to the 'copy' of Orsino's 'well penned' speech which Cesario has learnt, or, at Olivia's own literal insistence, the 'copy' of her own will.

239–56   Cesario changes direction, assuming she has penetrated the true cause of Olivia's resistance: pride. Her reiteration of Olivia's beauty suddenly, almost imperceptibly, prompts Olivia to share a

verse line (lines 241–3). Lines 244–5 may represent some of Orsino's
original message. Their tone is urgent, clichéd, and Olivia has heard
it all before. Her own verse reply expresses a new and measured clarity on her part, respectful but firmly direct. Cesario, still apparently
speaking on behalf of her master (her own veil throughout this
scene), enters further the imagined realm and, perhaps unwittingly,
perhaps deliberately, her language becomes hypothetical, that of
courtship (lines 253–6). Olivia encourages her to say more.

257–65 Cesario breaks out into the blank verse equivalent of an
aria, the greatness of which is inextricably bound up with its
dramatic power and texture. Imagining herself the lover of another
woman, she provides an extemporary and moving symbol of
passionate yearning. She would build a house of willow, write verse,
sing, and cry out. Her words and feelings of love would become inex-
tricable from either the day or the night, from the hills, and the very
air she breathes. The whole landscape would resound with her love;
Olivia would be changed by it.

There is a gradual crescendo of vowel sounds in this speech,
mixing the esoteric ('cantons' 'contemnèd'), the ordinary ('dead of
night'), and the extraordinary ('hallow' or 'halloo', both a sanctifica-
tion and a hunting call, and one which turns the mouth into the
shape for a kiss). These lead the actor (if he or she desires) to luxuri-
ate in each syllable of 'O-liv-i-a', a name able to move the whole
shape of the mouth, with its wide-open vowel ending. How far may
this *really* be Cesario's authentic female voice finding expression for
her attraction to Olivia? How far is it only the speech of a feigned
suitor on behalf of someone else (whose suit she does not, after all,
want to press very successfully)?

266–78 The half-line of verse before Olivia's potentially deflating
response (line 266) may suggest a pause and the reply itself cause a
ripple of laughter, or it may be spoken with breathless urgency on
the half-line with line 265. Olivia's nervousness, her own desire, again
interrupts Cesario's reply (line 269). Ever spirited, Cesario is perhaps
now trying to back-pedal, and may over-compensate by appearing a
little too petulant as she exits.

279–89   There could be a long and comic pause before Olivia's first line of soliloquy, a moment heightening her status as a dramatic character, and her relationship with the audience. 'What is your parentage?' recalls her reaction to Cesario's great speech, and she goes on to repeat his own words. Do we hear Olivia attempt a convincing impersonation of the object of her ever-emerging desire? 'I'll be sworn thou art' could sound as sexy and as head-over-heels as the actor chooses. Then Olivia begins to gabble; she's excited, cramming multi-faceted appreciation into a single line (line 282). 'Not too fast! Soft, soft' is a gift for the actor to slow down again, move position, to reflect, and ask two questions in two lines, perhaps pausing after each of them (lines 284–5), and vary the rhythm of the speech. She refers to falling in love as being like a 'disease', a plague (grimly resonant for Shakespeare's original audience), which may recall Orsino's earlier line about her purging 'the air of pestilence' (I.i.19). Not any more. Olivia's musing on the 'invisible and subtle stealth' of Cesario's 'perfections' may also echo Orsino's own appreciation of the power of music at the very beginning. She too is now caught up with an ideal object of affection, and one which she cannot ultimately have. And then she calls for Malvolio, providing an automatic contrast in tone.

289–301   Olivia's instructions could involve a comic reaction from Malvolio, especially in her asking him to run. There may also be some comic business with the ring. She may be thinking on her feet, and could be seen struggling to remove her own ring to convey to Cesario. She may not manage to give the ring to Malvolio until the end of her speech. Malvolio, laconically discreet, may suspect a change in his mistress's behaviour, but may also take her account at face value. We may catch a sense of Malvolio's foolish pride in what he perceives to be his mistress's abstinence. He may exit with absurd alacrity, or calm austerity. Olivia is alone again and speaks two rhyming couplets, conveying well her understanding of being caught up in a fate beyond her own control, and ending the scene with a moment of uplifting and high energy.

ACT II

Act II, scene i

0.1   It is not clear where we are for this scene: presumably, another part of Illyria. If it were to be recognizably a place that we have already seen, then the tensions of story and setting which here unfold could start to culminate in an exciting dramatic effectiveness. We may think we see Cesario enter with a stranger; if Sebastian were played by a boy (as he might have been for Shakespeare's original audiences), then the similarities would be even more marked. At closer quarters, through the defamiliarization of the ensuing dialogue and timbre of voices, here are two new characters. Their entrance and appearance will convey their relationship. Is one of them older than the other, suggesting more clearly a potentially paternal concern, or are they about the same age? The young woman's lost brother may remind us of her by his costume or his high social status; we've just heard Cesario say 'I am a gentleman' (I.v.269).

1–20   This dialogue in prose contrasts with what we have just heard. The opening lines suggest the voice of a follower, rather than of a leader; he probably enters last. The Cesario look-alike (he is probably unbearded too, suggestive of adolescence, or a fragile masculinity) uses awkward words: 'malignancy', 'distemper', 'recompense', 'determinate', 'extravagancy'. He forces us to listen afresh to an appearance with which we already feel familiar. We soon learn their names (line 14). This is a crucial moment of revelation for Antonio, who thought his companion was called Roderigo. A disguise is being removed. The twin's father sounds famous: Sebastian of Messaline. But we still have to learn Cesario's real name.

21–38   Antonio interjects with compassion, which may create space for some physical gesture the better to establish the kind of relationship which exists between the two of them. This private homosocial moment could include homoerotic undertones, or even be explicitly homosexual. Or, the relationship could be one of gentlemanly loyalty, of a kind servant serving his young nobleman. The moment also mirrors the first scene between the young woman and the Captain.

Sebastian draws attention to his sister's beauty. How alike are they? Who is the better looking? He wins our trust by talking of her 'fair' mind. Sebastian starts to cry, or holds back tears (lines 27–8). Antonio may offer him more nurture and drops a further hint about their relationship – 'if you will not murder me for my love'. It is easy for an actor to make Sebastian too lachrymose and, whilst the text supports this (lines 35–8), it may not readily win the audience's sympathy. But certainly there is scope to show a new and authentic masculinity in Sebastian's portrayal, though any self-indulgence on his part may be reminiscent of Orsino.

39–43   Alone on stage, Antonio breaks into verse. He is lyrical and mysterious, direct in the information he gives and withholds. His thought changes direction in the final couplet, which may lead to a change in his posture or movement too. He becomes defiant and carefree, pushing us ever closer towards catastrophe as he runs (?) off stage.

Act II, scene ii

0.1   Malvolio and one of the twins enter from different (or opposite) doors, according to the Folio stage direction.

1–16   Malvolio meets with Cesario, heightening the tension of confusion and possibly evoking a sense of the farcical so soon after the exit of Sebastian. Here we catch a glimpse of an imaginary, confusing perspective which may later be encountered by the play's characters. Malvolio may convey frustration, anger, and superiority through his way of walking; Cesario, perhaps lost in thought, does not want to be noticed. Prose is used for the crisp delivery of a message.

Malvolio's account of what Olivia wanted him to say (I.v.290–6) has absorbed his own particular tone. She neither made mention of a 'desperate assurance', nor suggested that Cesario never returned, nor asked to hear how Orsino received the ring. Does Cesario turn away from Malvolio's proffering of the ring (possibly around line 12)? It's equally possible that Malvolio is wearing Olivia's ring and may humorously struggle to remove it. How does Malvolio give up the ring? He could let it drop indifferently, toss it towards Cesario, or arrogantly throw it away. This moment of theatrical immediacy could be different in each performance and the action and reaction will be very revealing of the characters' feelings. How badly does Cesario want to retrieve the ring, for example? And in the theatrical moment, the actor must be ready to take it up from wherever it happens to land.

17–21   It is not clear when, if at all, Cesario does stoop to retrieve Olivia's ring. Likely places may be the beginning of her soliloquy, or lines 23–4, or even somewhere around lines 40–1. The actor may decide to retrieve it at a different point during each performance, depending on the moment. Cesario bursts into verse as soon as Malvolio leaves her, and could address the whole of her speech to the audience. She begins with an immediate pattering out of monosyllables, evoking Olivia's imaginary presence with the contrasting disyllabic 'lady' (line 17). There could be a pause for as long as the actor chooses at the end of line 18 as the realization bursts upon Cesario. She begins to piece together their earlier encounter. Further realization comes after a series of monosyllables until she reaches the staccato 'distractedly' (lines 20–1), a word which describes her memory of Olivia but also her own feelings at this moment. Her mind races forward in monosyllables (lines 24–5) and begins to break, making 'starts', as she has just said Olivia's did, in Act I, scene v.

22–41   Does the young woman laugh at any stage; is she holding back the laughter until any point? A release valve could be 'I am the man' or a pause before 'Poor lady . . .', when she may again take possession of herself with an expansive observation which can stretch out and occupy as much space as the actor wants (line 26). How far do we believe Cesario's pity for Olivia? How far is she genuinely upset at her realization about the 'wickedness' of disguise, or is she merely wistful? Suddenly, she seems to be speaking against her sex, stepping outside of her own femininity (or her own performed femininity, for the boy actor) to deliver a diatribe against women's fickleness (lines 29–32). She is full of questions and possibilities and, as she sketches her own situation, she arrives at a heightened sense of self-conscious awareness of the effect her appearance has on others (lines 33–9). But she too is desirous and, within Olivia's 'thriftless sighs', may also be Cesario's own. There are tonal echoes of Antonio's rhyming couplet at the end of the last scene, as Cesario abandons her outcome to time and the will of others.

Act II, scene iii

0.1 It is the middle of the night, and Sir Toby and Sir Andrew are drunk. The beginning of this scene may show them arriving back at Olivia's house, but they could already be discovered on stage to show they have simply stayed up late, and be well settled into their evening's drinking.

1–13 Sir Toby's call for Sir Andrew to 'approach' may gesture his companion over to where he is sitting, or swaggering. He may be offering him more to drink, inviting him inside, or he may want to speak to him confidentially. The actor could find verbal humour in trying to speak, and possibly slur, the Latin (probably a reference to the aphorism: 'to get up at dawn is most healthy'). Sir Andrew interrupts and his reply may be no less slurred. His diction seems direct, but in the end his utterance is a tautology. If he is struggling to speak, Sir Andrew's 'false conclusion' could get a ripple of laughter.

Sir Toby's 'unfilled can' may suggest that he is about to fill one himself by urinating. His brief moment of clearer thinking (lines 6–8) could occur while he is doing so. He again shows he is able to run circles around his companion. Sir Andrew's clottish reduction of Sir Toby's feed-line about the four elements (if Sir Toby is making water at this point, he could belch or fart as well, adding wind) reiterates the dramatic texture of this scene. It is one of immediate and spontaneous revels, an immediacy encouraged by companionship and the ordinary desire to escape responsibilities. Both want to feel supported by the other in that unspoken choice. Sir Toby introduces a full-stop to the dialogue (lines 12–13), and shifts our attention to the arrival of a third party. He calls for Marian (perhaps his drunk, familiar version of Mary) and wine (perhaps we've seen them run out of it).

13.1–36 The Clown enters instead. Has he just woken up, or is his imaginary context unimportant? It's rather as if their revels and verbal humour have conjured him as a dramatic inevitability. His mention of the picture of *We Three* may refer to a pub sign (the third in the picture being the drunk person looking at it), or a portrait (like the one of two fools and a jester's stick in the collections of the Shakespeare Birthplace Trust – cf. p. 29), or to a kind of trick picture, which plays on inversions and perspectives. To a modern audience it may carry the sense of 'if you only knew what we all looked like!' The Clown may even take a photograph of the three of them, or the line may refer to a sudden moment of stage tableau, with the Clown appearing from behind and in the middle of them.

In recollecting the Clown's fooling the night before, Sir Andrew tries to reproduce its effect and could stumble and struggle over the awkward, difficult words. It's pure nonsense, but Sir Andrew has a good head for it. We also learn of the sixpence Sir Andrew sent the Clown and here the Clown acknowledges the payment with further nonsense (lines 25–7). These absurd observations need no explanation. If spoken with conviction, their language, a mixture of physical descriptions, imaginary characters, a classical reference, and drinking, adds to the heady, drunken energies and the dramatic texture of the scene.

Perhaps words have moved into the realm of being merely sounds for Sir Andrew and Sir Toby, which makes them crave music, and give more money to the Clown to sing. Sir Andrew's joke about life being better without love (lines 33–6) may fall plaintively, and could lead to a distinct strain of melancholy, picked up by the song.

37–53 Various settings and versions of this song exist, some of which were edited by James Walker as an appendix to the multi-volume Oxford Shakespeare edition (1994). The Clown's song is a poem in its own right before being sung. Here, it is the first music required to be heard since Orsino's romantic opening speech, and it may convey echoes of those dying falls we heard earlier. It is a moment of suspension, of variation, an inset of emotional reality which may seep into the larger context. The Clown has everyone's rapt attention and sings about the ephemeral nature of love and the passing of youth. This will have different resonance for Sir Toby and Sir Andrew depending on how old they have been cast. Both seem without lovers, but perhaps Sir Toby is thinking of Mary. If so, how may the actor convey this? By looking at a photograph, or taking up some personal prop already associated with her: an item of clothing, a book?

How do the pair react to each other during the song? Perhaps they stare blankly into space, regretting the lost years: head back, eyes closed, with the world spinning tipsily? Or perhaps they are more obviously engaged and enthusiastic about it? The second verse reminds its audience to make the most of every passing moment. Sir Toby says the Clown has 'contagious breath', perhaps implying that the song was catchy, uplifting, or insistent in some other way. The Clown remains silent for nine lines afterwards, perhaps visibly savouring the song's effect, too, or maybe he's waiting to be paid.

54–67 Sir Toby suddenly brings a different energy to the scene. He called for a catch in passing (line 17), but now becomes more demanding, asking two long rhetorical questions and one short one (lines 54–7). Sir Andrew, of course, gives him immediate child-like encouragement, making a humorous boast at the same time ('I am a dog at a catch', lines 58–9). Sir Andrew may sing 'Thou knave' and start dancing as he does so. The Clown corrects him, again showing that he is in complete control (and probably not drunk) with the witty verbal patterning of 'knave' and 'knight' and the silly literal joke 'Hold thy peace'. The song could go on for as long as the actors feel they can sustain it. It may become gradually more and more frenzied as they continue. Perhaps they start making instruments of whatever happens to be lying around, and disturbing the order of the room. Two early settings for the catch are reproduced in an appendix to the Oxford Shakespeare.

67.2–80 Mary (Marian) enters, fifty-five lines after being first called to bring in wine (line 13). Has she brought any with her? She may initially go unnoticed above the 'caterwauling'. Her tone may be a reprise of the maternal care we saw her exercising over Sir Toby at the beginning of Act I, scene iii. He responds to her first. His mocking insults and self-justifications seem to burst from his irrepressible pleasure principle. Olivia is an extreme moralist ('a Cathayan'); they themselves are diplomatic ('politicians'). Malvolio is a sex-mad whore ('a Peg-o'-Ramsey': this phrase is so physical in its sound that it could be spoken with vitriol and be accompanied by some bawdy gesture); they themselves are merely three good old lads having a laugh ('Three merry men be we'). Again, Sir Toby may burst into song for 'Three merry men be we', and encourage the others to do so as well.

Whether or not an audience immediately understands these words is less important than the drunken exuberant energy with which Sir Toby may utter them. Sir Toby's prose is splendidly impressionistic at this point, leaping around, moving in different musical directions, which may invite some physical movement, too. 'Consanguineous' may be a real stumbling block for his drunken delivery. 'There dwelt a man in Babylon' could be sung to the tune of Greensleeves (as suggested in the appendix to the Oxford edition), and shows again how Shakespeare is pushing at the edges of dramatic prose to create naturalistic effects, but maintaining an internal lyricism and melodic mood throughout this moment of high spirits.

The Clown sits back to enjoy Sir Toby's comic histrionics (line 75); Sir Andrew lets out another of his momentarily scene-stopping boasts, unhurried and balanced, totally clottish and heart-warming (lines 76–7). And then Sir Toby, possibly, takes us as close as *Twelfth Night* gets to an explicit self-association with Christmas. We may hear a snippet of the old carol 'The Twelve Days of Christmas' (line 79), perhaps inspiring an even greater connection between the audience and these revellers. And Mary all this time has been trying fruitlessly to keep them all quiet and contain their exuberance.

80.1–9   Enter Malvolio. He might have appeared sometime before his actual intervention, incredulous, taking a mental note, and working up to his eventual explosion (which does not have to be shouted;

it could be spoken with quiet and chilling authority). Everything
stops and we have a chance to feel the powerful contrast of
Malvolio's puritanical interruption. In many productions he enters
wearing an absurd nightgown, but he does not have to. Perhaps some
of the revellers hide, freeze, exchange glances, or stifle uncontrollable
laughter. His word 'tinkers' may strike us as odd. Some productions
have these below-stairs revellers caught red-handed banging on pots
and pans in the kitchen. It's really just Malvolio summoning up a
gross insult, implying that they are worthless drunkards, or vagrants.
Sir Toby characteristically gives as good as he gets. If delivered with
the modern intonation of a swear word, 'sneck up' (go hang),
together with Sir Toby's undaunted audacity, could easily get a ripple
of laughter. He may even walk up close to Malvolio and say it.

89–105 Malvolio's next lines seem to be spoken mainly for his
own benefit, but they become just another excuse for Sir Toby and
the Clown to start singing. Mary and Sir Andrew may be seen, to
varying degrees, openly to enjoy the performance taking place before
them. Again, we may hear another song of the period: 'Farewell dear
heart' (see appendix to the Oxford edition). This moment may be as
protracted and as irritating to Malvolio as a production chooses. We
may see (more) dancing, competitive role playing, as clown and
knight recall song after song.

106–16 And then Sir Toby makes his retort for being called a
tinker. Drawing himself up we may see him spit metaphorical venom
for his insult to Malvolio: 'Art any more than a steward?' It is a dishon-
ourable remark, because it exposes the framework through which
Malvolio has no choice but to see the world, and make a living. 'Cakes
and ale' is wonderfully Anglo-Saxon in its tone, evoking an essential,
festive, and irrational world. It would make Malvolio's puritan stomach churn, as would the Clown's swearing by St Anne and referring to
the rich taste of ginger (also an aphrodisiac). Sir Toby's 'Go, sir, rub
your chain with crumbs' could again draw laughter when filtered
through the modern ear and thought about in its parallel, expletive
and sexual terms, but Sir Toby is also insulting Malvolio again about
his servant status. A third form of Mary's name is introduced: Maria

(she will be referred to by this form in the commentary from now on).

117–64   Malvolio immediately calls her Mary again, and may sound as though he were correcting Sir Toby. He may overhear her insult, and pretend not to, on his exit. She can achieve different comic effects depending on when, and whether or not, she pauses: 'Go *shake* your [pause] ears', for example, could be comically crude, and well received by the others on stage. The next few lines all lead up to the plot to trick Malvolio. Maria's remarks about the colour of Malvolio's beard, his legs, his gait, and his facial expressions may all be clues to the way in which we too have perceived Malvolio's comic physicality on stage. Perhaps Sir Toby and Sir Andrew are drawn towards him with rapt attention. The conspiracy between them is close, exemplified by the way Maria plays off 'ass' and turns it back to 'as' (lines 157–8). The Clown has remained silent for fifty lines (from line 110). Maria may appear to be including him in the plot, but what has he been doing all this time? Is he quietly observing, asleep, or drinking? Is his silence a sign of his becoming disconnected from the kind of foolery he sees emerging? He is not, after all, in control of it. The simplest solution may be for him to slip quietly away any time after line 110.

165–79   Sir Toby, Sir Andrew and the Clown are left alone on stage, but the latter remains mysteriously silent. Is he bearing out Malvolio's earlier insult that, 'unless you laugh and minister occasion to him, he is gagged' (I.v.81–2)? Their first few lines allow Maria to blaze a trail, with her admirers standing back amazed. Sir Toby, turning his attention indifferently towards his companion, asks a casual question: 'What o'that?' Sir Andrew's reply is not really an answer and instead allows the mood of general revelling to be momentarily, almost imperceptibly, punctured by melancholy. 'I was adored once too' cannot fail to tug at the audience's heart-strings with its lost sense of direction, and immediate demands for sympathy. That sudden, short line can open a gash of searing vulnerability for the character and the actor. It's equally possible that Sir Andrew remains blissfully unaware of any pathos, and may even say it proudly. If a production is interested in showing how desperate Sir Andrew is to emulate Sir Toby, then there may be a sense of one-upmanship.

How do the others react? The Clown is silent, but do we see any physical gestures of his sympathy or amusement? Sir Toby suggests that it's time for bed, and may appear not to have heard Sir Andrew's sudden expression of regret. Apparently ignorant of Sir Andrew's feelings, he twice asks him directly to send for more money (perhaps we have just seen Sir Toby run out of wine). Sir Andrew's agreement changes the mood, and the revels limp forward. The scene ends with an echo of its beginning, with the two men leaving the stage together, perhaps more slowly than the way they entered. If the Clown is still on stage he may follow them.

Act II, scene iv

0.1–13   It's likely that Orsino and Cesario enter from the opposite side of the stage from the members of the court. One of the main dynamics of this scene is how it gradually becomes more and more intimate as it unfolds and, by so doing, shows the effects of the private on the public. Orsino demands music, developing a contrasting dramatic texture to the previous scene. His request may seem urgent. Perhaps he is feeling the pangs of unrequited love again. We are back into verse and the contrast may make his commands and language seem heightened in their verbal structure. He continues his request to Cesario (we may recall that she originally envisaged using her musical talents in her post, I.ii.54–6), but his request is public enough, or addressed in more than one direction, for Curio to answer him. It is an 'old and antique song', and perhaps represents a particular kind of escape for Orsino. We learn that it was not Cesario who sang it (Is Orsino getting muddled in his self-absorption?), but 'Feste the jester'. Suddenly the Clown is named. His name suggests revels and feasting. Curio dares to mention Olivia and her father, whose taste for Feste's songs may explain why Orsino wants to hear an old-fashioned melody. Spending time with Feste is his way of seeing and hearing what Olivia sees and hears.

14–19   Perhaps the same musicians perform the same tune that

opened the play. The appendix to the Oxford edition contains a
setting which can be played twice under the ensuing dialogue, until
Feste arrives. His invitation to Cesario to 'come hither' perhaps indicates them moving down stage, withdrawing from the others into
their own private space. As in Act I, scene iv, a production could
explore the tension of whether or not the courtiers can overhear
them.

In addressing his speech almost paternally to the 'boy', Orsino is
really speaking to himself (lines 14–19). With Cesario's fixed attention, Orsino's self-indulgence could assume an edge of sexual charge,
and we may detect a whiff of flirtation moving in both directions. He
is asking for Cesario to remember him at some unspecified, future
date. When he introduces a discussion of true love into the dialogue,
he may be looking directly at Cesario.

20–40   Over the next few lines the pair of them share several verse
lines, fringed with possibility of subtext. Cesario carefully reflects
Orsino's romantic excess back to him by praising the music in terms
which Orsino may use himself (lines 20–1), and receives a compliment for so doing. We may feel the pain of Cesario's disguise as well
as being amused by her direct hints, which puncture and arrest the
flow of the dialogue. The half-line of verse (line 27) may be indicative
of a pause before Orsino continues, which means that 'too old, by
heaven' could easily get a laugh, even if played for melancholic effect.

Orsino has now effectively complicated and involved Cesario's
perspective on love with his own. His tone becomes more general
(lines 28–37), but still makes the occasion of it being particular advice
for Cesario an opportunity for Orsino to talk about himself. Cesario's
rhyming couplet could sound reticent, the rhyme closing up the
speaker, as well as the words themselves. It also provides scope for a
change of tone by effectively drawing a verbal line under an intimate
dialogue with the approach of Curio and Feste.

41–9   How does Orsino greet Feste when he arrives? He uses the
vocative, 'O fellow', which may express relief and a degree of familiarity. Orsino then curiously provides a context for the song we are
about to hear. It is sung by unmarried women and young girls; it is

explicitly feminine. He also emphasizes the song's innocent (silly) tone and says that it lingers on love's innocence. Feste may enter carrying a musical instrument, such as a lute.

50–65 Is this the song we were expecting? There is death and mourning, rather than the 'innocence of love'; it is about slaying the object of one's affection, or dying from love unrequited. Perhaps spinsters and maids used to sing it and be thankful that they had, as yet, escaped all the vulnerability and pain that love brings. But Orsino has not, and he seems especially to identify with the tune and regards it highly. The melody is probably slow and reflective.

How does Feste interact, if at all, with his on-stage audience? Does he sing the song directly to them, or out to the theatre audience? Is the imagined voice of the song female, given that it is sung regularly by women? If so, then Feste may direct 'slain by a fair cruel maid' to Cesario (if he's spotted her disguise). Olivia and Orsino have both been 'slain' by her, both been made to feel desire just beyond their reach. We may be able to perceive Cesario's grief for her dead brother whose 'poor corpse' she imagines is at sea, without any grave at all.

Is there any interaction between Orsino and Cesario during the song? Do we see them move closer together? They may sit or recline in some way, changing the mood of the scene from one of discussion, to one of awkward longing and anticipation. Are they being visibly changed by the music? Perhaps this is a moment when desire is struggling to make itself felt, in spite of how vulnerable it makes those involved. Degrees of homoeroticism may be perceived. Do we see, for example, Orsino daring to place his arm as if to put it around Cesario, perhaps inviting his page and confidante to lay his head on his breast? They may move almost as if to kiss, or they may actually kiss.

There is a sense in which Orsino may think that this is quite safe. Cesario is his servant and, moreover, a eunuch. This would, however, put into circulation a definite and complex homosexual understanding of how Orsino sees Cesario. If so, what may that do for how Cesario sees Orsino? Or, conservatively, it may mean that he has seen through her disguise, that she understands this and that what we have is simply an unusual, but enabling, fiction, controlled by patriarchal power. The words of the song act as a locus for the possibilities within the triangle of relationships (both hetero- and homosexual) between Orsino, Olivia, and Cesario. The dramatic moments which this one song can make possible make it an emotional nerve centre and a rich site of theatrical meaning. Desire, death, disguise, regret, pain, romance can all be made impressively present.

66–77 There is scope for further movement on stage between the end of the song and Orsino's next line. If Feste is using a musical instrument, he may play the music for a little longer without words; perhaps there is an awkward silence. Do we perceive what Feste's reactions are in response to what he might have seen taking place between Orsino and Cesario during the song? Orsino instigates a reaction first. It is a financial transaction, rather than praise, perhaps implying that the song has touched him too deeply for critical comment. The offering of money can often be protective, and keep emotion at arm's length.

Feste has enjoyed singing for them, a contrast to any pain and awkwardness that might have been portrayed. His quip can be as cruel as the actor chooses (lines 69–70), and he's already been paid, so he has nothing to lose. The 'doublet of changeable taffeta' may refer to Orsino's ambiguous or even troubled sexuality, and Feste's reference to the sea seems to crystallize an image of voracious and ubiquitous desire. It also reminds us of Cesario's brother again.

78–86 Perhaps Orsino is embarrassed, especially if Feste's remarks have been overheard by everyone else. Feste exits, making the mood shift back to the curious space of intimacy between Orsino and Cesario. Perhaps Orsino is trying to heal his vulnerability by becoming defensive (lines 78–81). The words of the song have affected him. Olivia is now his 'sovereign cruelty' (similar to 'a fair cruel maid', line 54), but he is still expressing his affection in abstract terms: 'fortune', 'miracle', 'queen of gems', 'nature' (made to work with the extraordinary verb 'pranks', meaning 'to adorn', in line 85), and 'soul'. Cesario responds pragmatically, daring to suggest a negative outcome, but Orsino cannot even admit this as a possibility.

87–109   Cesario now takes the imaginative initiative of encouraging Orsino to step outside of himself and consider his position in reverse, as the unrequited object of a woman's affections. Orsino's reply with half a line may indicate that he pauses before he reflects his self-sustaining fiction that women do not feel as much desire as men. He uses the language of appetite again in relation to desire, just as he did at the play's opening. Cesario tries to interrupt. He turns on her. She bravely tries to reason with him, and takes on the imagined perspective of her dead brother, allowing her to speak from both imagined and real experience. From Cesario's point of view, the fiction is possible because it is about her imaginary half-sister ('my father had a daughter', line 107). By making her reasoning sound like part of her autobiography, she can almost lift up her mask momentarily, urging its transparency with the careful rhythms of her speech, in a moment of heavy irony. Orsino is caught up in her narrative, catching her words on the half-line, and making the verse complete (line 109). He wants Cesario's full story.

110–24   Cesario's reply is one of the most painful speeches in all of Shakespeare. She starts with a 'blank', almost monosyllabic line about blankness and the absence of language, punctuated by the disyllabic 'never' to emphasize the negation of her imaginary half-sister. Unlike Orsino (at line 80), there are some loves of which it is impossible readily to speak. Cesario too is concealed, and we know that she feels the pain she is describing. Desire, far from being satisfied like hunger, fed on her sister. There is a critical, dispassionate tone in this awful observation with the hard consonant sounds of 'damask cheek'. The vowel sounds begin to open out more, and the language becomes softer; she is describing thought and the ultimate patience of waiting and waiting for love. Do we see poor Cesario smile on the line 'smiling at grief'; do we see her wipe away a tear, but laugh at herself at the same time, creating a bitter-sweet effect? She seems to have found again the tone of voice that she used for her 'willow cabin' speech (I.v.257–65), and seems enough in control of the moment to throw in a rhetorical question: 'Was not this love indeed?' Perhaps she adjusts her tone again to reiterate her disguise with 'we men', which could easily generate laughter.

Orsino's imagination is hooked. Perhaps he sees a parable of himself in Cesario's account. She replies enigmatically, as much for herself as for her master. Perhaps she is trying to fight back the tears by the time she reaches 'and all the brothers too', and she may protect herself by offering to do what Orsino requested forty-five lines earlier. He gives her a jewel, possibly another ring, echoing the one she has already received from Olivia. Cesario now possesses symbols of both their expressions of love. Do they leave the stage together or separately? One of them may stay behind, lingering in the pain and complexity of the moment, caught between bitter and sweet. The conclusion requires careful timing and sensitivity and will reflect back on the rest of the scene.

Act II, scene v

0.1   Sir Toby enters first, closely followed by a stranger and Sir Andrew. If the newcomer is of Olivia's household, he may be either a gentleman (he's called 'Signor', line 1), or a servant. The scene is set outside (as suggested by lines 14–15).

1–10   We learn the newcomer's name almost immediately: Fabian, which may be suggestive of 'reveller', or, according to classical history, someone who waits for the correct moment to strike, and then strikes hard. He's out to get Malvolio and his first lines suggest tenacity and the determination to enjoy himself. Professional theatres were never used for bear-baiting (though similar spaces were), so Fabian would, by his own admission, have been breaking the rules of the imagined and actual space (that is, Olivia's estate and the Globe theatre). Sir Andrew enters the dialogue ten lines into the scene; he offers agreement and encouragement, and has probably been visibly excited by the prospect of the trick before he speaks.

11–20   Maria enters. Sir Toby seems captivated and may be flirtatious. Maria has the pleasure of knowing that Malvolio is on his way. She also knows what is in the letter she has composed. What does 'the box tree' refer to (line 13)? It is essential that there is somewhere for the three men to hide, but somewhere from which the audience can see their reactions, as the scene unfolds. A box tree (perhaps too small a one) may be brought onto the stage, but there could easily be an obstruction of another kind: a wall, a bench, or some pillars, for example. The three men may hide just as Malvolio enters, emphasizing a mood of brittle, high excitement, or they may hide a little earlier and leave the stage to Maria as she places, throws, or drops the letter (how obvious is it in its placing and appearance?) for Malvolio to find.

20.1   How does Malvolio enter? He is absorbed in thought, but the opportunity for an actor to explore a range of comic possibilities is immense here. Perhaps he is very stately? Does he detect a sound, which he soon after dismisses? Perhaps, being utterly self-absorbed, he walks across the letter, or even stands on it, without seeing it. Does he speak his lines out to the audience, or more to himself? This would be a key opportunity for an actor to portray Malvolio as vulnerable in some way, perhaps as a helpless romantic. He doesn't think anyone else is around, after all.

21–6   It's ironic that we should hear about the occasion when Maria once told Malvolio that Olivia did regard him. The moment he refers to might have occurred recently, in terms of the imagined off-stage reality, in order to prepare Malvolio for such a moment as finding the letter. Shakespeare allows the actor every opportunity to emphasize egotistical traits with a cluster of '*mes*', '*mys*', and '*Is*' (for example, '*my* complexion'). Malvolio is indulging himself in emotional and mental masturbation.

27–77   Shakespeare now establishes the contrast and conflict of voices from different parts of the stage. Do Sir Toby, Sir Andrew and Fabian remain visible, watching Malvolio, or do they remain hidden, only appearing to make their brief interjections? Fabian's lines are longer, on the whole, and he is given some scope to accompany what he is saying with physical gestures ('turkeycock' line 28, 'blows' line 40, 'peace' lines 47 and 54, and later, 'woodcock' line 79, 'rank as fox' line 118). Sir Andrew makes fewer interjections, making their impact even more comic when he does so (lines 34, 74, 76, 86). Sir Toby is in danger of making too much noise throughout, which sets up the dynamic of Fabian consistently asking Sir Andrew and him to remain silent. The speed of these comic interjections is crucial to the overall pacing of the scene.

Although the fictional reality would never let them be discovered, an audience may be able to believe that the jest could collapse at any moment, and the conspirators be found out. We move from genuine exasperation on the eavesdroppers' parts when they hear him imagine himself 'Count Malvolio', which lasts until just before they realize that Maria's letter is having the desired effect. Malvolio's daydreams may lead to much physical gesture: he imagines himself in a velvet gown, making Sir Toby curtsy before him, and playing with his (possibly a pause loaded with sexual innuendo) 'some rich jewel'. The Folio text, though, does not seem to allow for a pause here and prints 'with my some rich jewel'.

We may, when we are alone, imagine ourselves making utterances to those we think we dislike most; Malvolio imagines scolding Sir Toby and warning him against drunkenness. Sir Andrew endears himself again by responding warmly and fully to hearing himself called a 'foolish knight' (line 73; compare note to I.iii.23–40). But these conflicts and comments have merely been spinning out the anticipation until Malvolio sees the letter (line 77).

78–90   The audience is now further drawn into the anticipation of the three in hiding. Perhaps he holds the letter as he might contemplate a precious stone. We hear his first impressions. It's Olivia's handwriting and, for good measure, there is a bawdy joke, too: her 'c's, her u's, and her t's', calling to mind 'cut' or 'cunt', just as Malvolio is on the brink of breaking open the seal of a letter and enjoying its contents. Fabian or Sir Toby may use a bawdy gesture to explain the joke to Sir Andrew. The mention of Lucrece on the seal itself reminds us of rape. Olivia is being mentally raped by Malvolio and he himself is being mentally raped by Maria and her fellow conspirators.

90–118   Malvolio is reading the letter for the first time and may exaggerate the metre of its verse. He may clumsily pronounce 'know' to rhyme humorously with 'who'. He is very conscious of verse and prose and mediums of communication ('the numbers altered', lines 96–7). The pleasure and humour of these next moments is in hearing and seeing Malvolio become more drawn into the riddle as he perceives it, and struggling to make sense of 'M. O. A. I', suggestive enough to be a hint towards 'Malvolio', but just beyond satisfying interpretation. The letters, if said slowly, can make it look as though the actor is preparing to bestow a kiss; he may even try to pronounce them as a word in their own right.

Fabian's lines about 'Sowter' (lines 117–18) are obscure to any modern audience: a good bloodhound will not lose a scent, but in Malvolio's case the scent is strong, so there is no cause for concern that the jest may not work. These lines are also part of the turning point when the eavesdroppers begin to stand back and enjoy the joke taking effect.

119–68   The pun on 'revolve' (to turn physically, as well as to encounter a sudden change in thought) is part of the in-built motorized energy of the scene. If the three men have become overconfident, they might have come out from hiding and have to return suddenly before Malvolio turns and sees them. The letter is rhetorically shaped (lines 135–7, 140–1, 142–3), but also contains strong visual images that we may see Malvolio begin to re-enact here (lines 143–5, 156–60, 164–8). There is ample space for the actor to build up to a great comic climax of revelation.

We may see any number of reactions and silent interventions from behind Malvolio during his reading of the letter (lines 131–68), but this part of the scene is a gift to the actor playing Malvolio. We may see him being blindly trusting of the fake letter and absurd in his romantic expectations, a humorous counterpart to the tone set by Orsino. From line 151, the audience may enjoy the contrast between Malvolio having read the letter, and being addressed directly by him. There is a further sting of enjoyment as we learn of a postscript (line 163). Malvolio may exit with great urgency, as he rushes towards consternation, or he may leave in a stately and controlled way, oozing self-satisfaction and puritanical self-control.

168   The three men come forward. They are probably reeling in excitement and feeling the relief at being able to laugh openly about what they've seen and heard.

169–96   The men's reactions encompass total admiration for Maria, which may lead to an exaggeratedly subservient welcoming of her. A hierarchy of appreciation may be established, with Sir Andrew following Sir Toby in imaginary gestures of tribute to Maria. Sir Toby's summation (lines 182–4) puts plainly his hoped for outcome. It is made up of monosyllables, except for that one crucial word, as far as Malvolio is concerned, 'image'. These words widen out into open vowel sounds: 'run mad', which the actor could say as slowly as the mood of self-congratulatory exuberance warrants. The audience looks forward to a conflict between Olivia's melancholy and Malvolio's hopelessly misplaced flirtation (a comic counterpart to Olivia's own for Cesario).

The ending of the scene has Sir Toby elevating Maria to the status of a devil in classical mythology, 'to the gates of Tartar', which could here indicate the presence of something sinister and serious in this jest. Sir Andrew seems to exit last, following Sir Toby, Maria and Fabian off stage. Perhaps he is even left behind momentarily, enjoying the jest slightly later than the others, and then runs to catch them up. Shakespeare has prepared the way for one of his greatest of all comic scenes, and we can look forward to seeing the plot laid here coming to fruition.

ACT III

Act III, scene i

0.1   Cesario arrives a second time to take Orsino's suit (and his jewel) to Olivia. She encounters Feste. Do we see instant recognition between the two of them? Does Feste ignore her, or stare at her disconcertingly?

1–10   Cesario makes a pleasant remark to him, which suggests he might have been playing his tabor from the beginning of the scene, or taken it up suddenly on seeing Cesario. In production this scene often marks the beginning of the second half. The music at this point could remind us of Act 1, scene i, as well as Feste's earlier songs. His reappearance emphasizes his absence from the gulling of Malvolio.

Cesario knows him from just two scenes before. They share rather a laboured joke (lines 4–7), but one which usually generates laughter. Cesario's dialogue with Feste is the first time we have heard someone else engaging with him almost on his own terms. Cesario is quick witted and is ready with replies for him. This establishes a unique relationship. How far does Feste appreciate this, or is he superior, perhaps out of defensiveness? It's appropriate that the two characters in disguise (Feste by the fact of his motley, however that may be made manifest) should be able to talk fluently with one another.

11–29   Feste's first attempt at an unanswerable statement compares the pliability of language to the soft leather of a cheverel (kid skin) glove (Shakespeare's father was a tanner and glove maker). Cesario develops this remark, moving forward from Feste's 'turned outward' to 'wanton'. Feste brings both his original statement and Cesario's together by mentioning a real or unreal sister. Is this his way of hinting that he knows Cesario to be a woman, or even that he knows about her brother? Without a name, his sister would have no word connected to her which could be dallied with, therefore she would remain chaste. There could be a bawdy pun here, if 'wanton' were to be pronounced 'want one'.

Feste's next attempt at an unanswerable remark is more successful. Words and their truth are weakened because of written legal bonds (lines 19–20). Now Cesario disengages slightly from Feste's wit; she may break the momentum of their dialogue by adjusting her posture. She becomes more literal and straightforward with him (lines 21, 25–6, 30 and 36). Feste may be seen and heard to make a rather nasty reply ('I do not care for you') in response to Cesario's apparent affability (lines 25–9). Do we see (or have we seen) any reason why Feste should say that he does not care for Cesario? This may hark back to the way he saw Orsino and Cesario during 'Come away, death'.

30–40   Feste's enigmatic association between fools and husbands, pilchards and herrings may suggest that he thinks there is something fishy going on, but it's also his way of saying that husbands are bigger fools than he is himself. He then explains the hallmark of his own foolery; he is a 'corrupter of words' and omnipresent, since his foolery is possible wherever language is. The actor playing Feste needs to be able easily to elide meanings and use words like objects ready to be kicked around. Feste's gnomic 'I think I saw your wisdom there' may refer to I.v.160–210 and/or to II.iv.41–77 (the only other times they have been on stage together), or to some other imagined moment. Has he seen through her disguise to her true female self, 'her wisdom'?

41–58   Cesario tries to leave, perhaps suddenly feeling insecure. She gives him a coin. Feste wishes she had a beard, either to improve her disguise or, scornfully, because Cesario is a eunuch. It is a moment of tension and Cesario makes light of it by suggesting she does want a beard, but the beard of someone else, playing on 'want' as both lack and desire. The range of possible meanings in this moment is considerable. First, Cesario may be confirming that she is a eunuch and simply doesn't want a beard (that is, it's impossible for her to have one). Secondly, Cesario implies that as a eunuch she wants someone else's beard (which may then put into circulation a freely admitted homosexual desire on Cesario's part). Thirdly, she confirms her true female identity to Feste and also her trust (a trust which may be increased by casting Feste as female, as some productions do, against the text). Whatever the interpretation, Feste now extracts more money from Cesario, possibly by way of a bribe, or even blackmail. Cesario's secret is safe so long as Feste receives more money.

His remark about Troilus and Cressida also puts into circulation several possible meanings. It may relate to his seeing through Cesario's disguise and telling her that he sees her as both male and female. If Cesario pays him, Feste will act as Pandarus and help her disguise to remain. Or, he may play Pandarus and help her to win Orsino's affections (as either a man or a woman), or it may simply be his own convoluted way of asking for more money (the most obvious primary meaning). Cesario's 'I understand you, sir, 'tis well begged' is the opportunity to clarify the meaning which performance makes possible. Feste has the last word as he leaves to tell Olivia that Cesario has arrived. His apparent doubt about 'who you are and what you would' (another allusion to 'What you will') may convey either genuine or false confusion, or it may carry with it something of 'Your secret's safe with me.' He leaves the stage emphasizing his ability to step out of words, and change their shape, perhaps having amused the audience into a more heightened critical and verbal awareness.

59–67   Finishing off her encounter with Feste, and forcing the audience to reflect upon his kind of fooling, Cesario has her second soliloquy, for which she breaks momentarily into verse, the effect of which may create a sense of distance and contrast, reminding us of the romantic underpinning narrative. She has observed Feste observing her, and this in itself may support the reading that he has seen through her disguise. Her speech reiterates Feste's wisdom (lines 59, 65, 66), until its final line when she realizes a contradiction: Feste's wisdom is tainted by being only used for fooling. Cesario finds her resolve again and puts herself back in control after the uneasy dialogue from which she's just escaped.

68–81   Sir Toby and Sir Andrew may bring onto the stage something of the same comic exuberance that they had when they last left it (II.v.197). Here they encounter somebody new. They may see him as handsome, well to do, thoughtful and poised. Sir Andrew's French may aim to intimidate him and put him to the test. Cesario's immediate response forces Sir Andrew to slip back into English, probably taken aback and made to feel unexpectedly nervous. He does not speak again to Cesario in this scene and remains silent for fourteen lines. Sir Toby also tries to have nothing to do with the stranger, urging him to go into the house as soon as possible (lines 73–4). Cesario may seem as if she were taking Sir Toby to task, and being pert; Sir Toby may reply with amused indifference (lines 75–81).

81.1–91   They are interrupted by the arrival of Olivia and Maria. Immediately Olivia enters, Cesario breaks into a formulaic greeting. Sir Andrew may make his comment of naive admiration to Sir Toby (lines 84–5) as an aside out to the audience, or to himself. Cesario's greeting is exactly what Olivia wants to hear, but she may be seen to be especially and secretly delighted by the reference to her 'own pregnant and vouchsafed ear'. Sir Andrew's absurd extraction of what he sees as the key adjectives may even lead him to make a note of them in a little commonplace book.

Olivia changes the mood of the scene directly when she asks the other three to leave her alone with Cesario. Maria has said nothing in this scene. Is there a garden door as part of the set, or does Olivia imply this is part of the imagined off-stage reality? In any case, it must be closed, and we suddenly learn that we are out of doors. Now the tone becomes one of dangerous confidentiality. It's possible that Sir Andrew and Sir Toby may contrive to stay on stage to overhear the secret conversation about to take place. They may even hide again behind the same box tree.

92–104   The two women break readily into verse. Olivia does not yet know Cesario's name, a reminder of how important nomenclature is in *Twelfth Night*. Cesario replies by calling Olivia 'princess', an exaggeration which serves unintentionally to flatter, rather than distance. Olivia mentions Orsino and thus keeps him present in this gradually emerging threesome. Cesario tries her best for Orsino and emphatically reminds Olivia of her own servant status (lines 99–100). Olivia is insistent though and completes Cesario's half-line of verse (line 104).

105–20   We enter the poetry of someone who is perfectly smitten and for whom the voice of the beloved has become like the 'music from the spheres'; and Olivia will not allow Cesario to interrupt *her* (line 108). Olivia's language embraces magic and mysticism, referring to Cesario's last visit as an 'enchantment'. Perhaps Cesario tries to answer Olivia's questions and interrupt her speech as it unfolds, before Olivia embarrasses herself too much. Olivia slips again into an enigmatic language of evasion. She refers to a 'cypress, not a bosom' hiding her heart. As well as the obvious primary meaning of a see-through veil, Olivia also places herself unintentionally within the poetry of the play, reminding us and Cesario of Feste's song about 'sad cypress' in Act II, scene iv.

121–33   Cesario's reply is bald, direct, and truthful: 'I pity you.' But even this is seized upon by Olivia and pushed beyond its immediately transparent meaning: 'That's a degree to love.' What is the physical relationship between the two on stage at this point? Does Olivia remain courtly and restrained, or does she make any bold advances? Does Cesario dare to turn or back away from the Countess? She restates her position more poetically, contrarily (lines 122–3). Olivia's 'Why then, methinks, 'tis time to smile again' can be delivered with pathos, as well as hope. It is many mooded, and it does not convey quite sufficient conviction for us to believe in Olivia's ebullience. There could be pain lurking at the back of it, of which the statement is self-aware.

Olivia's next lines seem to evoke further self-pity. She pulls rank on Cesario's social status, accusing him of pride, but insulting him in the next breath. Cesario is a cunning wolf, rather than a brave and kingly lion in her eyes. It is extraordinary how suddenly we encounter comparisons from the natural world of survival. But civilization returns with the striking of a clock (line 127.1), and Olivia's direction changes. She voices her resolve not to bother Cesario any more, but in the next breath expresses her regret, and envies his future wife. 'Westward ho!' would have signalled to audiences at the Globe that, in the imagined off-stage reality, Cesario was departing to cross the river Thames, following the line of the Strand.

134–46   Cesario makes to leave, but Olivia cannot resist. She must know more. Lines 137–40 are made up entirely of monosyllables as the two women quickly exchange self-knowledge and perceived reality. Cesario's 'Then you think right, I am not what I am' could be delivered as an aside, and cause a ripple of ironic laughter. There is frustration for both characters; on one side a desire to control, on the other a desire to escape. Olivia's next few lines may be delivered as an aside, but do not have to be, and if overheard may make Cesario justly angry.

147–62   Olivia's rhyming couplets are possibly an expression of her becoming more and more overwrought. She names Cesario, perhaps forcing the other to move. Although Olivia's speech refuses to permit contradiction, her last rhyming doesn't scan properly (line 154). Her thoughts seem to be flowing more quickly than she can find language to express them. She knows her love is unsought, but believes it better for being so: an illogical and untenable position. Cesario replies in rhyming couplets. She is trying to speak the same language, trying to make herself understood. To Olivia's ears these may seem like strange excuses. What does she hear when Cesario says that 'no woman has' his heart? Is the emphasis on '*no*' or on '*woman*'? Cesario goes on to qualify the statement (lines 157–8) and vows never more to represent Orsino's love. Cesario perhaps moves to leave here, finishing the scene on a rhyming couplet. But Olivia rhymes, too, with her last words of desperate self-persuasion. Does she follow (even chase) Cesario off the stage, or turn reluctantly from him, pausing first for a moment of regret?

Act III, scene ii

1–15   Three of the comic revellers enter and we shift suddenly back into prose. We may be expecting more about Malvolio at this point, but focus shifts to Sir Andrew, who may even have a packed suitcase with him. Sir Toby and Fabian could be in pursuit of him, trying to slow him down and explain. Toby's 'dear venom' (line 2) is his way of making light of what could now be Sir Andrew's exaggerated passion, based on a few moments of exchange between Olivia and Cesario (III.i.86–91, unless we saw him overhear any more of their conference). Sir Toby's tone may become more affectionate as he encourages Sir Andrew, calling him 'old boy' (line 7). Fabian's interjection seems improvisatory, and Sir Andrew is initially doubtful; Sir Toby offers mock endorsement.

15–27   Fabian delivers a key speech of persuasion, which may involve some physical contact with Sir Andrew to emphasize his case. 'Dormouse valour' may be a joke on 'dormant'. Fabian's advice is amusing because it requires an altogether different Sir Andrew, one who can speak with dazzling wit in order to win over Olivia. His reference to an icicle on a Dutchman's beard is visually striking and absurd in its illustration of Sir Andrew's imagined hopelessness. It compares to Sir Toby's earlier observations (I.iii.96–8) and serves to reiterate Sir Andrew's gangly appearance.

28–49   But it works, for Sir Andrew seems to be flattered and we detect glimmers of hope (lines 28–9). His humorous preference for 'valour' is presumably because 'policy' would require too much intelligence on his part. Sir Toby contributes an improvised and comic persuasion, introducing a further comic episode (lines 30–5). A pause before 'eleven' (line 32) may raise a laugh as we see Sir Toby thinking on his feet, possibly even appealing to Fabian for support. Fabian offers further encouragement, and Shakespeare is making full use of a three-way dynamic of encouragement and new directions (lines 36–8). Sir Toby's urgent and exaggerated advice about how Sir Andrew should write (lines 39–45) could also involve physical gesture and contact. His companion needs no more convincing after this speech and may even seem to be in a hurry to get away. Sir Toby's deliberately affected use of 'cubiculo' (Italian for bedroom) reiterates the tone of mock heroism and romance in which Sir Andrew's intentions have been thoroughly caught up.

50–61   Fabian can't wait to comment upon Sir Toby's power over Sir Andrew, 'a dear manikin'. Sir Toby is open about his own cynicism, turning an affectionate 'dear' into one describing the amount of Sir Andrew's expenditure which Sir Toby himself has enjoyed. The two plotters look forward to the fruits of their sport: the letter from Sir Andrew, his cowardice, the ultimate reluctance to fight, and the expectation that the Count's youth (they do not know his name yet) will not offer any strong retaliation.

62–78   Maria interrupts and shifts the focus (one of her characteristics). She has urgent news, and may be seen hurrying onto the stage, perhaps laughing cheerfully, hence Sir Toby's reference to her being 'the youngest wren of nine' (line 62). This is a good example of an eighteenth-century editorial emendation. The Folio reads 'mine', which may more reflect Sir Toby's affection for her, as well as his desire to control the jesting, and indeed Maria herself. The audience has the satisfaction of sharing some of Sir Toby's and Fabian's pure delight to hear that the jest has worked. Her eye-witness account continues and Sir Toby or Fabian may even imitate Malvolio's smiles with eager anticipation. Sir Toby's gesture for Maria to lead the way may convey gratified flirtation on his part, and the three characters probably leave the stage in haste. This short scene has set in motion future revels and reported the coming to fruition of an earlier one.

Act III, scene iii

0.1 We last saw Antonio and Sebastian about 700 lines earlier in Act II, scene i, about forty minutes ago in stage terms, or longer if the production has an interval. Shakespeare's care in naming them when they first appear is crucial in establishing them as key narrative and dramatic presences.

1–14 Perhaps Sebastian leads them both onto the stage, echoing the earlier scene; Antonio is still in pursuit. They seem to be in the middle of an intense discussion (if not an argument), the impact of which is strengthened by its contrast in verse coming immediately after the prose of Act III, scene ii. Sebastian has been chiding his friend, and may now appear more resigned and accepting (lines 1–3). Antonio explains why he is following Sebastian: 'desire, / More sharp than filèd steel'. Does this make Sebastian seem humbled, conciliatory, more tender? Does this lead to any (further?) indication of whether there is any sexual attraction between them? Taken out of context, Antonio's speech (lines 4–13) could sound like a love poem, pledging duty and loyalty.

14–24 Sebastian takes up Antonio's speech on the half-line; his repeated thanks may be suggestive of embarrassment on his part. Sebastian's translating his deep gratitude into monetary terms (lines 14–17) perhaps serves to reiterate their status as master and servant. He changes the subject: it's a foreign place so why don't they become tourists for a while? Antonio suggests going to their lodgings instead. In his reply, Sebastian reveals that the scene is set during the daytime (line 21), and repeats his previous suggestion (lines 22–4).

24-37   But Antonio interrupts him on the half-line and urgently reveals his true reasons for not wanting to wander around these streets. He explains to Sebastian and to the audience why he has 'many enemies in Orsino's court' (II.i.40). Sebastian's reply shows just how much like strangers these two really are. He did not know about the battle, but his knowledge of Antonio thus far leads him to believe that he would have been bloody in conflict (line 29). Antonio's explanation hints ambiguously at piracy. His city repaid what they took from Count Orsino (lines 33-5), but Antonio did not.

37-48   Although Sebastian immediately reflects back (on the half-line) concern for Antonio's safety, he appears to leave. Antonio is prompted to give Sebastian some money (possibly the fruits of his piracy). His suggestion that they meet up later at the Elephant refers to an inn/brothel close to the Globe theatre, and would have had special topographical resonance for the original audiences. A production may choose to substitute 'the Elephant' with the name of a well-known local pub. It is unusual to see the servant give money to his master and the word 'purse' is re-iterated until the end of the scene, especially with Sebastian's casting himself as Antonio's 'purse-bearer' (line 47). They quickly go their separate ways, sharing an unrhymed, final line of verse, and may leave on opposite sides of the stage. Sebastian and Antonio are now separated and in Illyria, with the possibilities of death on one side, and confusion on the other.

Act III, scene iv

1-16   Olivia and Maria enter, perhaps suggesting a scene of domestic intimacy. Do we detect any of Maria's earlier excitement (III.ii.62-78) in her swift reappearance? The Oxford edition marks Olivia's opening remarks (lines 1-4) as an aside, but she could be speaking openly to Maria about Cesario. She is clearly deeply preoccupied and absorbed in her thoughts of Cesario and their next meeting. Olivia's 'I speak too loud' (line 4) may signify that she thinks she is being overheard by Maria, or be an admission that she is simply speaking too boldly.

She asks to see Malvolio because his morose humour will help her to re-capture something of her former self. Nothing could be further from the truth. Her repeated 'Where's Malvolio?' (lines 5 and 7) serves as a comic overture just before his entrance. What we are about to see will further overturn Olivia's sense of her own domestic space and present her with an absurd image of one-directional desire (like her own for Cesario). Perhaps Maria can scarcely keep her countenance when she replies (lines 8–9), but her words here and a few lines later serve finally to herald the moment of high comedy. Olivia speaks in verse and Maria in prose. Not only does this emphasize their social status, but it relates to their different narrative agenda at this moment (romance and revels). Maria goes to fetch Malvolio, and Olivia just has time to speak a reflective rhyming couplet (lines 14–15) curiously identifying herself with Malvolio's 'madness' because of her own conflict of feeling simultaneously both sad and merry. At what point precisely does Olivia see Malvolio? Perhaps she becomes aware of his entrance while she is speaking, and turns to see him; perhaps lines 14–15 are spoken as an aside in response.

17–26   The entrance of Malvolio, carefully anticipated and plotted as it is, can raise one of the biggest laughs in all of Shakespeare. Like a well-oiled motor, Malvolio's entrance is like turning on the ignition to create a sudden and inevitable chain reaction of responses and outcomes. How yellow are his stockings? Does the cross-gartering look uncomfortable? Is he in pain? How much of his legs do we see? He enters believing himself to be the most desirable object that Olivia could possibly encounter. Hearing her 'How now, Malvolio!', he makes sure that his first line rhymes with it: 'Sweet lady, ho, ho!' He is ingratiating himself verbally as well as visually.

He is smiling absurdly, just as Maria has already observed (III.ii.73–4), which here represents a gross visual contradiction to Olivia's mourning habit: his 'sweet' with her 'sad'. His ingratiation continues with his echoing her last word, and repeating it. Perhaps his physical posture changes as he refers to his stockings, absurdly and awkwardly in terms of a medical symptom (lines 19–20). He sounds at once capricious and nonchalant, but is able to state his purpose directly through referring to love sonnets.

How closely does Malvolio approach Olivia? Her interjection and two short questions could be delivered with genuine concern (line 23). His position becomes even more exaggerated when he refers to the colours so prevalent on stage: black is his mind, his gartering and, possibly, Olivia's dress. Line 25 could be delivered as though it were Malvolio's great attempt at a flirtatious joke. If we call to mind that yellow and black were the colours on Shakespeare's coat of arms, this moment works visually to remind us, perhaps self-mockingly, of the biography of the author. Malvolio enigmatically shifts to use the third person, 'it' and 'his' (line 25). The extended joke is that he thinks he is making perfect sense and being flirtatiously confidential by talking to Olivia through hints and allusions.

27–36   Olivia's 'Wilt thou go to bed, Malvolio?' comes out of nowhere and needs only to be delivered with the concern of 'I think you'd better have a lie-down' for it to raise much laughter. There may be a slight pause before Malvolio responds, perhaps just long enough for him to raise his eyebrows and change his expression to one of eager delight. To his ears, Olivia loves him so much that she has just suddenly invited him to have sex with her. His reply is a line of an old ballad, so we may hear the snippet of a song here, dramatically echoing the snippets of songs we heard from Sir Toby and Feste in Act II, scene iii, while they were misbehaving in front of Malvolio himself.

The implied stage direction for him to kiss his hand could be done in a courtly fashion, perhaps accompanied by a bow, or we may see something much more sexually provocative and even slightly disgusting at this point: a slow licking of fingers perhaps? Whatever the actor chooses to do, he repeats the action enough to provoke Olivia's next question. Maria also interjects. She's been a silent but animated observer since Malvolio entered (for the last twenty-two lines), and may be trying to take the focus off Olivia. Malvolio either ignores her (ironically assuming it's none of Maria's business), or his obsession makes him quite simply deaf to everyone apart from Olivia.

37–53   The dialogue is propelled along by Olivia's short questions (except line 44, which could be delivered as an aside, a prayer, or even shouted out imploringly). These interweave with Malvolio's quoting from the letter. Perhaps rather endearingly for the audience, he's committed what he believes to be Olivia's words to memory. We could hear and see him quoting them with self-satisfied, masturbatory relish, blind to everything but his own pleasure, and possibly echoing our first seeing him read the letter. Or, he may genuinely seem to be seeking her approval, with varying levels of desperation. Olivia's climactic 'Why, this is very midsummer madness' could be exasperated, annoyed, pitched highly, and be in further response to Malvolio having made a physical advance on her. Olivia could say it to the audience, possibly signalling that we are *just* teetering on the edge of farce. If she were to scream and run away from him, we could be tipped over the edge.

54–60   Here is a lull and break in the action, a pause for breath, as a servant interrupts. Cesario has returned to see Olivia. Why? What can she still have to say? The news may strike a contrasting, physical change in Olivia and provide her with an escape route from the current situation. Her exit lines ironically deliver Malvolio up to the hands of his tormentors, Maria (the formal usage perhaps more readily expressing Olivia's commanding tone) and Sir Toby. Her instructions for 'special care' may sound tender and momentarily soothing. However, there may also be an anxiety on Olivia's part to keep Malvolio away from Cesario.

62–80   Alone on stage, Malvolio enjoys a privileged relationship with the audience, rather as he did in the eavesdropping scene. His thoughts are articulated through a plastic prose which stretches and accommodates them easily in lists and subordinate clauses. He moves from the thought of Sir Toby, feeling the compliment of his attention ('no worse man'), and relates the opportunity to the letter (II.v.140). In his recollecting the physical descriptions of how he should appear, Malvolio may try some of these out in front of us (lines 70–1). 'I have limed her' ('I have caught her') strikes with crisp irony, since it is he who has fallen into the trap. And then he brings God ('Jove') into the equation. A bad interpreter of texts and a puritan here utterly misplaces his belief, convincing himself with an ill-founded sense of fatalism. It is this logic (which includes refining and repeating the slow, purring, comic sound of 'scruple') which reiterates for us just how locked within his view Malvolio actually is (lines 75–9). He is just thanking God when we see Sir Toby, Fabian and Maria enter to torment him further.

81–91   All three probably feign an air of concern. Sir Toby's first line introduces a sense of urgency. Where is Malvolio when they discover him: momentarily far up stage, or perhaps obscured from them by some item of set design? Fabian's 'here he is' may actually be genuine (Malvolio could initially be out of sight), or it may be just his way of interrupting Malvolio's musings. Here are three against one, an echo (without Sir Andrew) of the eavesdropping scene. They may position themselves on each side of Malvolio, or surround him.

His status is proudly independent and he could move away from them before they intrude too much on his personal space, or he may push them rudely aside (lines 86–7). The word 'discard' implies he thinks of them quite literally as items of rubbish. Maria may sound shocked and scared (lines 88–90). Her mention of the 'fiend' may draw a further physical response from Malvolio, or he may ignore it. The moment is moving towards an attempt at exorcism. Malvolio's ear pricks up on 'my lady prays' and he becomes immediately interested. These words seem to have achieved a momentary connection, but he seems deaf to all else.

92–101   Sir Toby's intervention changes the tone to one of quiet gentleness, almost as one may speak to a child, or to a domestic animal. Perhaps Fabian and Maria look fearful and stand slightly apart as Sir Toby tentatively approaches Malvolio. Sir Toby's voice could change, with sudden aggression, making Malvolio, Fabian, Maria, and the audience jump (lines 94–5). Is he attempting to start the exorcism? Malvolio's reply shows he is now definitely listening, but he may speak out of incredulity, rather than desperation. Maria and Fabian may move closer to Sir Toby and Malvolio (lines 97–9). She may cross herself when she mentions praying; by contrast, Fabian's intervention is much more basic and physical. She cleverly mixes further irritation of Malvolio with flattery (lines 100–1). Malvolio obsessively picks up the word 'lady' and translates it into 'mistress'. Maria clearly knows which keys to press.

102–20   The tempo of three different interjections pushes forward the rhythm of this moment as Sir Toby ostensibly tries again to take control, which Fabian now echoes and supports (lines 104–7). Sir Toby's usages of 'bawcock' and 'chuck' (lines 108–9) are both inappropriate: the former may be used to a close friend, the latter by a husband to a wife, or a parent to a child. His exaggerated social register serves to arrest Malvolio and for the first time makes him almost speechless (line 110). He is becoming gradually more exasperated. Sir Toby then tries to coax him and draw him close like a hen (line 111), and again contrasts this by talking immediately about Hell, and mentioning Satan for the first time.

Maria may seem desperately concerned: 'get him to pray' may even encourage Sir Toby to push Malvolio to his knees. Her tone may change in reply to Malvolio's retort, to sound suddenly regretful, or even matter of fact (line 117). Malvolio may be seen to draw himself up. He has allowed himself to become irritated, and he shouldn't have. Recalling the letter's advice to be 'surly with servants' (II.v.140–1), he carefully separates himself from their company. His language is balanced and poised, but his exit lines could just as convincingly be bawled out as spoken with restrained defiance and fragile calm. Crucially, he looks forward to more clashes in the future.

121–36   Perhaps there is a delicate moment of suspended animation just after Malvolio has left the stage, before the three of them burst into a fit of hysterical laughter. Sir Toby is incredulous, but sets the tone for the others' reactions. Maria wants them all to follow Malvolio, and she may move to leave the stage, or encourage the others to lead the way. Fabian's short line becomes emphatic through its dominant use of monosyllables and open vowel sounds: 'why, we shall make him mad indeed'. This line stands out from those around it because of the way it strikes us acoustically. The audience may begin to feel a distance growing between themselves and the revellers. Maria's hope that 'the house will be the quieter' may not, so far as we have seen, be strictly true. Sir Toby, Sir Andrew and Feste (where has he gone to?) will still make lots of noise. Sir Toby's directions bring a decidedly darker tone to the imagined possibilities.

'Come, we'll have him in a dark room and bound' has a drum-like, rhythmic quality. It is definite, absolute, and sounds sinister. His plosives carry him along: 'pleasure', 'penance', 'pastime', 'breath', 'prompt'. These sounds may indicate a careful delivery, but they also ripple with energy and inevitability as Sir Toby already sees the future of Malvolio's torment. Does Sir Toby kiss Maria as he mentions crowning her 'for a finder of madmen', for example, or perhaps imitate the action of placing a crown on her head? She may be about to reply, but is interrupted by a sudden change of direction.

136.1–66   Sir Toby notices Sir Andrew's approach first. He enters carrying a paper. Fabian's interjection could be spoken either to Sir Toby, Maria, both, or out to the audience. If Sir Andrew hears him, he seems not to understand the true degree of relish with which Fabian may deliver a line full of 'mmmm' sounds (line 137), like someone enjoying a good meal. Sir Andrew sounds pleased. Perhaps we see Fabian take the paper from him first on 'Is't so saucy?', an energetic pun which may prompt some stage action on his part. Fabian's joke seems too subtle for Sir Andrew, whose facial expression may change from agreement to bewilderment (line 141). Sir Toby takes (snatches?) the letter and begins to read. Perhaps he imitates Sir Andrew's voice whilst reading the letter. A short double act begins between Sir Toby and Fabian. We get to hear Sir Andrew's words read out with as much humour as the actor playing Sir Toby is willing to contribute; we hear and see Fabian's reactions (at once both ironic and encouraging of Sir Andrew), and we get to see Sir Andrew's reactions. He remains silent, but perhaps we see him mouthing the words as Sir Toby reads them. This would be another illustration of Sir Andrew being a 'dear manikin' (III.ii.50) to Sir Toby.

167–77   Maria has said nothing since line 129. She could be listening, watching and enjoying the scene before her. Dramatically she could give an important energy to the scene by facing her reactions out to the audience. Sir Toby motors the action forward by encouraging Sir Andrew to seek Cesario directly with what probably appears like mock ferocity: 'swear horrible' a 'terrible oath', and with a 'swaggering accent'. Perhaps these words are accompanied by physical encouragement of some kind, or even by Sir Toby drawing his sword and showing Sir Andrew how he should look. Sir Toby's 'away' (line 176) may be accompanied by a suitable gesture. Sir Andrew, silent for thirty-six lines, suddenly leaves, with a mind made up and preoccupied.

178–89   Sir Toby explains to Maria and Fabian what they should do. Perhaps we see him tear up the letter (line 178), as he looks forward to the duel between Sir Andrew and Cesario. He recognizes Cesario's good breeding and anticipates his opinion of Sir Andrew: one of excellent ignorance (line 182). Perhaps Sir Toby and Fabian play at killing each other, with looks like cockatrices, for the amusement of Maria (line 189)

189.1–93   Olivia and Cesario re-enter in mid-conversation (which we last saw in Act III, scene i). The *exeunt* marked in most editions for Sir Toby, Fabian and Maria is not in the Folio, and the three may even hide again in the box tree (if we see the same set before us as Act II, scene v), or withdraw out of sight whilst perhaps still overhearing what is being discussed.

194–210   We suddenly enter the private, romantic sphere of verse again after about 160 lines of prose. Olivia is monosyllabic and direct on her entrance, and is talking about her own earlier responses to Cesario. Her embarrassment and insecurity continue (lines 196–8). Perhaps Cesario is following awkwardly behind her. Cesario again reflects back to Olivia Orsino's own feelings. We then see another jewel or ring change hands. This is the second one that Cesario has received from Olivia (the first via Malvolio in Act II, scene ii), and the third she has received in total (the other being the one that Orsino gave her in Act II, scene iv, to give to Olivia). This one, though, contains a portrait miniature of Olivia herself. Perhaps Cesario tries to refuse it, or backs away just before 'refuse it not' (line 202).
   Olivia gives Cesario a double-tongued instruction to return, and makes herself vulnerable by talking about her virginity (probably all the time wishing that Cesario would deflower her on the spot). Their

shared line of verse brilliantly conveys both giving (on Olivia's side) and giving back (on Cesario's side, line 208). Olivia asks Cesario for a second time to return tomorrow and, bizarrely, if not humorously, compares him, in an emphatic rhyming couplet which marks her own exit, to a 'fiend' who takes souls (her own included) to Hell.

211–49   We slip back into prose. Sir Toby calls Cesario 'thee', making clear the master–servant relationship; Cesario responds with 'you'. Sir Toby does not name the attacker, and his descriptions jar comically with what we already know of Sir Andrew: 'full of despite, bloody as the hunter [. . .] quick, skilful, and deadly'. Cesario's body language and facial expressions may help to express gradual worry and change; she is now in serious trouble. She tries to leave to find Olivia, and perhaps starts to exit. Sir Toby may restrain her in some way (line 237). He continues to contradict the off-stage reality. Fabian (who has probably been quietly enjoying the dialogue for the last thirty-eight lines) is put in charge of Cesario.

250–63   Cesario seeks confirmation and is met with even worse news, comically abbreviated by Fabian: 'all I know is that your challenger is so angry with you that he wants to kill you' (lines 251–3). Cesario's panic is gradually becoming more apparent and intense. The audience can now begin to imagine Sir Andrew starting to quake in the off-stage reality as Sir Toby addresses him about Cesario. Do Fabian and Cesario leave the stage (line 263) as directed by the Folio text? Many productions choose to keep them both on stage so that when Sir Toby says 'Fabian can scarce hold him yonder' (lines 271–2), we can see Cesario struggling to leave, which Sir Andrew misinterprets as an advance.

264–99   Sir Toby and Sir Andrew may enter quickly to add to the mounting comic tension. They probably move downstage and to the side in conversation. If Fabian and Cesario were to leave the stage, however, we would have an emphatic, parallel moment of persuasion with Sir Toby claiming to see things off-stage which Sir Andrew cannot. Perhaps there is some (by now familiar) physical contact between the two men: Sir Toby showing apparent concern for Sir

Andrew, Sir Andrew looking anxious and hanging onto every word.
Perhaps Sir Andrew starts to leave, too (line 270). There is a momen-
tary return to that particular comic naivety that is one of Sir
Andrew's hallmarks. Like a child he proffers the idea of giving
Cesario his own horse, grey Capilet, in order to placate him.

Sir Toby moves away from Sir Andrew and towards Fabian (who
might have remained on stage, or who has just re-entered with
Cesario, line 279.1). There could be a balanced stage picture before us,
Sir Andrew and Cesario on opposite sides of the stage, facing out to
the wings, out to the audience, staring or stealing glances at one
another, while Sir Toby and Fabian talk in the central downstage
area, and cross to each other's opposite side, sharing the joke of the
situation confidentially.

Cesario's bawdy joke ('little thing' playing verbally on penis, lines
290–1) is probably turned out to the audience, and can release some
of the laughter as we head towards the comic climax of the duel. Sir
Toby crosses again to Sir Andrew to encourage him and to enjoy the
anxious, final preparations of his companion, whilst leaving Cesario
alone with hers.

299.1–308   Antonio enters, perhaps towards the back of the stage.
He pauses, watches, and sees Sebastian about to fight a duel with a
tall gentleman. The comic moment between the mutual fear of
Cesario and Sir Andrew is suddenly given the added energy of a
different perspective and the possibility of a new direction.

Cesario's explanation (line 300) may be spoken as an aside to Sir
Andrew, or it may be uttered in fear and be audible only to herself
and the audience. They draw their swords and the moment of silence
during which they stand and hold them, waiting for each other to
make the first move, can last as long as a production dares. Does one
of them start to fight? If this is Cesario then the audience's sympathy
and admiration for her may well increase.

Antonio rushes forward, probably with his sword drawn, and
interrupts either a fight about to start, or one which has just started.
Their fight could be as exciting or as perfunctory as a production
chooses. He also brings the energy of verse back onto the stage. He
rushes to Cesario's defence (lines 301–4), but Sir Toby intervenes. He's

just had his sport interrupted by an interfering stranger. Perhaps Sir Andrew and Cesario hold their ground for a little longer. Three swords may be seen drawn in the course of lines 301–6, and then Sir Toby apparently draws his and starts to fight with Antonio. This contrast of masculine readiness throws into further relief the expressions of cowardice and worry we've just watched unfold for about 80 lines. Sir Andrew and Cesario may part to opposing sides and give centre stage to Sir Toby and Antonio, or they could remain frozen in terror and let the new action take place around them.

308.1–22   At least two officers enter and Fabian either shouts a warning to Sir Toby, or tries to stop the fight before the officers do. They bring rationality on to the stage. Cesario takes the initiative of asking Sir Andrew to put his sword away (lines 311–12). She may win the moral high ground by this and even appear mockingly forgiving with 'if you please'. Sir Andrew takes Cesario's suggestion as literally benevolent, rather than in any way expedient, and makes some comic reference to the horse he promised (lines 275–6), a promise Cesario never actually heard. Antonio is recognized and arrested. Perhaps we see him being tied up or handcuffed. The officers do not appear to be concerned with the other three, all of whom had their swords drawn when they entered the stage.

323–49   Antonio speaks to Cesario, thinking she is Sebastian. She is confused and 'amazed' at his asking her for money (lines 325–8 and 330). The fact that she doesn't recognize him means that Antonio can't have known Sebastian until after the shipwreck. Antonio knows he will be led away to his death, and there is the added tension of the officers trying to take him away as quickly as they can. Cesario thinks Antonio is only asking for a loan and offers him some money of her own, half of what she has with her, on the spot (lines 335–7). Antonio's 'Will you deny me now?' can be one of the saddest lines in the whole play, and in his lines which follow, we hear him realizing that he's been confounded. Cesario's more expansive denial interrupts Antonio's half-line of verse (lines 342–7) and is expressed in abstract terms. Oddly, 'babbling drunkenness' may remind us of 'babbling gossip' in her speech of imaginary love to Olivia back in

I.v.262. Antonio may utter a cry of complete despair, and the officers again try to remove him.

350–5   Antonio humbly requests 'to speak a little' in spite of the officers, and we hear an account of his journey to this point in miniature. The tone of this moment is utterly serious and could be truly poignant depending on how we have seen his relationship with Sebastian depicted. His language is urgent as he stares his own imminent death in the face, with phrases such as 'jaws of death', 'sanctity of love', and 'devotion'. The officers are necessarily and uncompromisingly indifferent, offering a consistent and contrasting frame to Antonio's desperation (line 355).

356–69   Cesario hears her dead brother named by Antonio. She may start suddenly, begin to stare, or gesture towards him. Perhaps we see her remaining silent out of emotional paralysis, or for her own safety. Antonio is taken away by the officers, perhaps looking back to Cesario all the while. She speaks to herself, or out to the audience, as soon as he's gone. Perhaps there are tears in her eyes as she begins to articulate her feelings of high hope and wonder, in rhyming couplets (lines 364–8). The dramatic texture of this heightened moment is juxtaposed with Sir Toby's ordinariness (though Sir Toby ironically says he and his companions will do what we've just seen and heard Cesario doing: 'whisper o'er a couplet or two of most sage saws', lines 368–9). Sir Toby, Sir Andrew and Fabian also allow more prominence to her continued utterances by tidying the stage and grouping together.

370–5   A curiously dizzying effect may be achieved. By commenting on hearing Sebastian named for the first time, Cesario also speaks his name for the first time. She may be affected physically by it and appear dazed; she may start to cry. Perhaps she struggles to get the words out. Her duality of grief and amazement mirrors her own imagined reflection of herself and Sebastian 'living in my glass' (line 371). 'For him I imitate' refers to her appearance as his double, and also the possibility that she has been wearing his clothes all this while, originally salvaged from the shipwreck. When a twin dies, the

survivor often self-consciously embraces further his or her characteristics in this way. On her exit line about the saving power of
tempests and the ocean, we see both Cesario and Sebastian leave the
stage in one figure; we are borne back to the beginning of the play,
and the imagined reality of their separation.

376–86   Sir Toby is unrelenting in his pursuit of sport and returns
us immediately to prose and the atmosphere of revels, reiterating
Cesario's cowardice, and encouraging Sir Andrew to follow and
strike him. The stupid Sir Andrew can't wait to do so and exits mid-
sentence (line 384). Fabian and Sir Toby clear the stage with different
expectations of what they may and may not see.

ACT IV

Act IV, scene i

0.1–22   Sebastian could enter just a split second after the end of the
last scene, sustaining the tension. There is an echo of the beginning
of Act III, scene i, with Feste talking to someone he thinks is Cesario.
We last saw Feste about half an hour ago in performance time, and
his first line implies that in the imagined off-stage reality Olivia has
asked him to request that Cesario visits her. She presumably cannot
wait to see him again (as she herself suggested only about ten
minutes ago in the last scene: III.iv.209), and is full of longing.
    Sebastian turns, irritated, and replies in curt verse (stopping on the
half-line). He will not be drawn into Feste's prose ramblings. Feste,
too, may well be irritated. The last time he spoke to Cesario, he was
in control of an extended and witty dialogue, hence 'well held out,
i'faith' and his lines of comic negation (lines 5–8), comic because it's
true: he's talking to the wrong man. Perhaps Sebastian moves to leave
during Feste's speeches; perhaps he is followed around by him, stop-
ping to turn and deliver his own retorts. This could happen differently three times during lines 1–20, and provide a comic and urgent
visual rhythm to the scene.
    Feste's play on 'vent' may lead him to do an imitation of Sebastian,

who he also suggests is affected and, possibly, foppish (a 'cockney'). Sebastian, like Cesario, doesn't have a beard, a point that Feste remarked on earlier (III.i.43–4), perhaps leading to this further slight on Cesario's masculinity, as well as suggesting that there is an air of femininity about Sebastian. We see Feste being offered money (line 18), but explicitly not for his fooling. He appears perfectly delighted by it nevertheless (lines 20–2).

22.1–30   Sir Andrew suddenly appears with Sir Toby and Fabian, interrupting Feste. Before Sebastian has even had time to register the arrival of these strangers, Sir Andrew approaches him and hits him. This may be only the slightest of taps, and cause a ripple of laughter. Sebastian responds by hitting Sir Andrew three times (line 25), which could be done with great force, perhaps even striking him to the ground. His line 'Are all the people mad?' reiterates the rich conflict of tones and clash of contexts which this scene has presented thus far. It also helps critically to distance us from the antics of the revellers. Sebastian may draw or even use his dagger, as some editions suggest (because of lines 27–8 and 38), but he does not have to. Sir Toby intervenes, and Sebastian may strike him as well. Feste leaves to call Olivia, pushing the energy of the moment forward to resolution, if not further confusion.

31–42   Sir Toby's 'Come on, sir, hold' suggests that Sebastian is struggling hard to escape from Sir Toby's clutches, or striking him, too. Sir Andrew has recovered enough to make a pitiable statement of his illogical intentions. Sebastian's 'Let go thy hand' suggests a further struggle on his part. 'Put up your iron' may refer to Sebastian's sword or dagger, which he has drawn since the fight began. Lines 39–40 suggest that Sebastian has escaped Sir Toby's clutches, and turned his drawn sword on Sir Toby instead. They begin to fight, possibly quite fiercely, before Olivia interrupts.

43–9   The fighting stops. Sir Toby and, by implication, his two companions are reprimanded. They may try to interrupt, but Olivia holds her ground and orders them to leave. What are Sebastian's first reactions on seeing Olivia enter? Perhaps he is arrested by her beauty and authority. She turns to call him Cesario, and seems to continue straight on with her speech before Sebastian has time to reply.

49–63   Alone with Olivia on stage, Sebastian is suddenly given the singular attention of a woman of high rank who is a complete stranger to him. Her characteristic directness is intensified by the quarrel and the situation. Sebastian's reply picks up on Olivia's final couplet rhyming 'me' and 'thee', and we hear him rhyme for the first time (lines 58–61). His associating 'stream' with 'dream' connects with the stream and dream-like quality of the poetry he is here given to speak. He sounds as if he is surrendering himself to a new way of talking, of being. During lines 58–61, we hear 'dream' twice, echoing on either side of his line of surrender. The internal rhymes and echoes of the long vowel sounds (bound by the two successive rhyming couplets) 'dream', 'stream', 'steep', 'sleep', 'Lethe' (Leethey), and 'still' produce an hypnotic effect. Olivia's reply shows that she has recognized a change in her Cesario, and they leave the stage sharing a line of verse, making the sound of the final rhyming couplet together. Their shared dreams have begun.

Act IV, scene ii

1–11   The location is unclear. Maria enters with Feste and asks him to put on a false beard and a gown. Unless these items are discovered as part of the set design, either she or Feste carries them onto the stage. To whom does 'him' refer (line 2), and why must Feste hurry? Perhaps Maria is referring to Sir Toby as she goes to fetch him. Feste is alone on stage. This is his first soliloquy, and he's talking about play-acting. Perhaps we hear him trying out his Sir Topaz voice (lines 7–11). It is also a brief moment of anticipation and his calling Maria and Sir Toby 'the competitors' could lead us to expect a game of some sort.

12–17   Does the way in which they enter suggest any development in their relationship? Sir Toby shares in the game immediately he enters, perhaps indicating that he has set it all up, and that Maria was merely obeying his instructions. Perhaps she helps to put the finishing touches to Feste's disguise. Feste replies in a dog-Spanish. He's mocking a Roman Catholic priest. Sir Toby and Maria probably hear and react to his Sir Topaz voice (lines 13–17).

18–49   Suddenly, the audience is informed about what is going on. There is a prison of some sort (perhaps under the trap-door, or implied behind another door, or built into part of the set). Sir Topaz is visiting Malvolio, another cruel joke. Do we see Malvolio in his 'dark room and bound' (III.iv.130)? Whether we do or not may alter the degree of pity we may feel for him. Does Malvolio see Sir Topaz at any point as the scene unfolds? If he does then it implies either that Feste's disguise is quite convincing, or that Malvolio's state has seriously affected his judgement. This, too, could instil pity. Feste's word play and mock exorcism as Sir Topaz (lines 26–7) may amuse Sir Toby more than Maria and are counteracted by Malvolio's descriptions of his condition and where he is: 'hideous darkness' like 'Hell' (lines 31 and 36), fearing for his sanity (lines 30, 41 and 48).

50–71   Malvolio is sounding increasingly desperate, persistently irritated by someone he assumes is trying to help him. The cross-questioning about Pythagoras is a dramatic echo of Feste's catechizing Olivia in Act I, scene v. When Sir Topaz bids Malvolio farewell (line 60), perhaps the prison hatch (trap-door, or other opening) is closed, and Malvolio screams. Sir Toby is congratulatory and satisfied in his praise, but Maria observes that Malvolio could not see Feste. This may or may not be true, but the disguise was essential, because he might have done.

Sir Toby's next few lines seem confidential and confessional in tone. He sounds tired of this extended joke and regretful of Olivia's anger. But what may he mean by 'the upshot'? The death of Malvolio, or his complete mental breakdown? The Folio gives an exit for Sir Toby only (line 71.1), so Maria may stay on stage with Feste. If this decision is made, then Sir Toby may direct his exit line to her, hinting at a later amorous liaison (line 71).

72–118   Feste bursts into song about his lady who 'loves another'. Malvolio's cries of 'Fool' (lines 74–8) are as much about himself as they are interruptions and calls for Feste's attention. Feste probably opens the prison hatch again, either during the song, or as late as line 80. Is he still wearing his gown and beard, or perhaps he removes them during the song? What difference is there, if any, in the way that Malvolio speaks to Feste as opposed to Sir Topaz? Certainly his manner towards Feste has changed: 'good fool' (lines 81 and 85). How far does Feste enjoy this second chance to torment Malvolio? Perhaps he throws his voice or moves when he is convincing Malvolio that Sir Topaz has returned to speak with him again (lines 95–102). His repetition of 'I will' creates a pun on Topaz's 'Marry, amen', mocking the liturgy, but also subtly reminding Malvolio of the wife he can never have. The mood of the scene may gradually change towards one of relief as Feste acquiesces in Malvolio's humble requests.

119–32   At what point does Feste close the prison hatch again? Perhaps when Malvolio asks him to be gone (line 120), or maybe at the end of the song. If the latter, then the song may be entirely directed towards Malvolio. The song could be sinister and nasty; it could be vindictive and angry, even if its melody sounds sweet. A final spurt of vile bitterness could be expressed towards Malvolio at the end of it. We may see Feste dancing on top of the trap-door, as if it were Malvolio's grave, for example, conjuring more Hell and darkness around the prisoner with the references to the 'Old Vice' and the Devil. There may be a frenzy about the song, the scene even becoming differently lit to convey 'rage' and 'wrath'. Feste leaves (with or without Maria if she's still on stage), and Malvolio is left alone as present–absent on stage, alienated and in the dark, and perhaps a little more hopeful than he was earlier in the scene, but that depends on the reactions and behaviour of Feste.

Act IV, scene iii

1–7   Sebastian enters. His first lines bring immediate contrast to the awful plight of Malvolio that we've only just witnessed. A production may even juxtapose the two characters in a more obvious way: Malvolio may call to him from his prison, for example. Sebastian especially notices the sun, which a production could use to show, through the lighting design, that we have now reached the beginning of a new day. Or, if the action appears to be continuous, the staging is limited, and Sebastian's observations are not literally bodied forth, then the language works harder on a metaphorical level, and we glimpse instead Sebastian's own interior moment. He draws attention to a pearl that Olivia has given him (probably a ring), the third she has given to her Cesario, as far as she is concerned. Is he celebratory, incredulous or merely bewildered? 'Wonder' (line 3) can be variously interpreted. Like Malvolio, we hear him state explicitly that he is not mad (line 4). How unhappy he would be, if only he knew the truth about Antonio! For Sebastian, ignorance is bliss.

8–20   His thoughts develop in soliloquy. Is he moving around, patterning the stage with his mental musings, or is he speaking out directly to the audience, or a combination of both? Lines 9–16 would sound just as true if they were spoken by Malvolio; we've just heard and seen his version of similar sentiments. Sebastian could even deliver these lines directly on the trap-door, or close to Malvolio's prison. The reasons Sebastian finds for Olivia not being mad follow closely on one another in a single sentence (lines 17–20), suggestive of a speedy vocal delivery.

21.5–35   Olivia enters with a priest. Is this the real Sir Topaz? The moment again helps to establish powerful echoes with the darker scene of torment immediately before this one. Olivia's first line suggests impetuosity, perhaps even a burst on to the stage with contrasting, pragmatic energy: 'Blame not this haste of mine.' Her speech is at once an invitation to marry and a confession about her own 'jealous and too doubtful soul'. Is there a comic pause before Sebastian's reply? He, like us, has just heard about a wealthy and attractive future, and it's been offered to him on a plate. He pledges his allegiance in a couplet; Olivia replies in another couplet which is both a direction for the priest to lead their departure, and a prayer for blessing. Do Sebastian and Olivia kiss? Has Sebastian grown in confidence and self-assurance since the beginning of the scene? There may be a comic moment of 'I can't believe my luck' if he glances out to the audience as he's led off.

ACT V

Act V, scene i

1–6 Feste enters carrying, and possibly reading, a letter. Fabian follows closely behind him, perhaps trying to snatch it from him. Feste could be taunting Fabian with it. This is the first time we have seen them on stage together, and the moment suggests a familiar relationship. The beginning of the scene presents an arrested moment of their pursuit, the object of both their interest, a letter, 'his letter', possibly the one recently written by Malvolio after Fabian took him paper and ink (IV.ii.117–18). We do not have to understand the obscure, possibly contemporary allusion (lines 5–6) to appreciate that Feste has an important prop about him, of which the significance may become clear later.

6.1–9 Orsino enters with Cesario and members of his court. This is the first time we have seen him since Act II, scene iv: that's at least forty minutes in performance time, or even as much as an hour (if there's been an interval). In Orsino and Cesario, we perceive a mirror image of the couple we've just seen leave the stage a few seconds before. He does not know Fabian, so his opening question suggests that he wants to know if 'Lady Olivia' (notice his re-iteration of social status) is in the vicinity. Orsino's calling them 'friends' may be his way of being controlling and familiar. Feste's retort, 'trappings', verbally pushes away Orsino's familiarity, which he tries again in the next line with a fuller acknowledgement of the Clown (line 9).

10–43 In the repartee which unfolds between them (the first time Orsino speaks in prose), Feste protests that his foes are better for him than his friends. Is the actor's delivery of these lines about self-knowledge in any way different from his other moments of fooling? Do we think momentarily of Malvolio here (lines 15–20)? Orsino appears to enjoy Feste's explications, and may encourage the rest of his court and Fabian to do so as well (line 21). Perhaps Feste holds out his palm for payment (line 23), or else Orsino gives it to him unprompted. The joke is that having established himself as Orsino's 'friend', Feste then proceeds to extract more money from him. Feste's lines authorizing 'for this once' the instincts of flesh and blood (lines 28–9) may be a barbed observation about Orsino's relationship with Cesario (taking us back to Act II, scene iv, when we last saw all three of them on stage together). Orsino is easily won and pays Feste again. The reference to 'the bells of Saint Bennet' could lead Feste to sing 'one, two, three', like a descending scale of bells being rung (lines 34–5). Orsino suddenly seems to realize Feste's cynical exhortation and denies money a third time (line 36). Feste leaves and Orsino eagerly anticipates the arrival of Olivia. Cesario is probably looking increasingly uncomfortable at this prospect.

44–59   The mood suddenly changes with the entrance of the officers with the arrested Antonio. Do we see further glimmers of hope from Antonio as he sees his Sebastian (Cesario) again? It's clear that Cesario has told Orsino all about the episode. Orsino's language returns to his familiar verse, but there is a new robustness in it. The masculine language of war is full of obstructive sounding words: 'besmeared', 'baubling vessel', 'bulk unprizable', 'scatheful grapple' (lines 46–50). The First Officer's thumbnail, historical sketch recalls the actual names of ships, and real people dismembered in battle (lines 55–7). There is an immediacy about it, touching Orsino directly by recollecting the suffering of his nephew.

60–86   There may be a further exchange of looks between Cesario and Antonio: Antonio lachrymose, resentful, confused; Cesario, sympathetic, kind, desperate. Cesario's intervention works, because Orsino gives Antonio the chance to explain. Antonio is ready with an immediate reply, and interrupts him on the half-line, whilst showing him due respect: 'noble sir'. His speech is an expansion of his earlier, shorter explanations (III.iv.350–61) and as such constitutes the first honest and openly direct speech, confirming love and duty in a public arena, that we have heard thus far in the whole play. It is a critical appraisal of the events which the other characters, apart from Cesario, lack. This may be the first time that Orsino has heard about the shipwreck.

87–91 Cesario's openly simple question 'How can this be?' is followed immediately by Orsino's question of Cesario, or the officers, immediately off-setting Antonio's directness with more confusion. Antonio's reply interestingly reveals the time-scale of events since the shipwreck: three months, making his sense of betrayal even more keenly felt.

92–105 We are just beginning to push towards a possible revelation when Olivia and her attendants arrive, perhaps including Feste, who went to fetch her. Orsino's instruction to the officers to take him aside helps to tidy the stage (on which there are now at least eight people, counting named roles only), and establish some deliberately framed observers (the silent Fabian making another one of these, who has apparently remained on stage since line 6).

This is the first time we have seen Olivia and Orsino in each other's physical presence; both have until now only imagined each other (as far as the audience is concerned). She may enter with vigour, even defiance. She has Cesario (Sebastian) and no longer wants Orsino's attention. Suddenly she sees Cesario before her. Is Olivia angry, surprised, incredulous? Both Cesario and Orsino attempt to speak. She seems to ignore Orsino, and Cesario hints that Olivia should listen to her first (line 102). Olivia's reference to music may stir in us a recollection of the opening scene and of how Orsino's daydreams of Olivia were all caught up in his sensuous delight in the music. How different is the reality now staring him in the face!

106–34 They are an equal match for each other: he making a sudden accusation, she turning it around to self-praise. From what Orsino says, it sounds as though he is nearly confounded by her. His devotion has led him nowhere. Olivia remains firm and reflects back to Orsino his freedom of choice. She may be regarding Cesario just as much as Orsino during these exchanges. Orsino seems suddenly full of threats and may advance towards Olivia when he talks about killing what he loves out of jealousy (lines 113–16). His speech operates like a smokescreen, and sounds much more violent than its substance really is. The violence is only part of Orsino's rhetoric. He is doing no more than taking Cesario out of Olivia's sight. His use of

the words 'sacrifice' and 'lamb' may suggest a paternal interest in
Cesario (with its allusion to Abraham and Isaac), 'raven' may be
appropriate if Olivia is still dressed in black. His threats end in a
rhyming couplet, declaring his love for Cesario. This could sound
like music to Cesario's ears; its effect makes her reply in rhyming
couplets. All those present on stage hear a young man saying that he
will love an older man more than ever he could love a wife, and more
than his own life (lines 130–2). Moreover, this pledge is made to
heaven, too (line 133), and could sound highly intimate in its intonation.

135–59   The tables have suddenly turned on Olivia since her
entrance. She feels acute alienation since Cesario is genuinely ignorant of her pleading and unaware why 'the holy father' is being sent
for. Orsino and Cesario start to leave again. Perhaps we see them
both turn, on Olivia's 'husband', a word twice reiterated by Orsino
and heard three times in all (lines 139–41). Olivia's further intervention (lines 142–6) is oddly reminiscent of the letter Malvolio received
('be not afraid of greatness', II.v.135). The Priest enters to confirm that
Olivia and Cesario (Sebastian) have married in the off-stage reality
only two hours earlier. His metrically full lines bring a brief sense of
calm and order. What are Olivia's and Orsino's gestures towards
Cesario during the public sharing of this news? Perhaps they seem
momentarily united in their confused and demanding interest. There
may be a short pause at the end of the Priest's final half-line of verse,
as Orsino registers the news.

160–7   He is the first to react, and starts what should be a private
conversation with Cesario, but one which here becomes a public
reprimand. Perhaps we even see him push Cesario towards Olivia
(lines 164–5), and start to leave again. Cesario's brief attempt at
protestation seems to be made in light of her feelings for Orsino,
again immediately complicated by the intervention of Olivia. The
stage picture here may be one of Cesario being trapped between an
angry master and mistress, her status and safety very much now at
stake.

167.1–83   Sir Andrew enters suddenly, crying for help. We may just have time to imagine Sir Toby's wound in the off-stage reality. How severely hurt is Sir Andrew with the blow across his head? His familiar childish tones may be heard in his pathetic wish to be at home (lines 167–73), and his news is touched with malapropism: 'incardinate' (to make a cardinal) for 'incarnate'. He doesn't see Cesario immediately, so the staging at this point needs to be carefully handled. He could enter from the opposite side of the stage and, in his dazed pain, and the replies he makes to Olivia, not see Cesario until Olivia turns her attention to him (lines 177–8). Sir Andrew may genuinely cower before the vision of his attacker. He speaks to Cesario rather as a spoilt child may make excuses for bad behaviour: you really hurt me and someone else made me do what I did. Cesario's rational explanations burst out confidently in contrasting verse (lines 181–3), with Sir Toby trespassing on the very end of them.

183.1–95   Some editions have Feste re-entering here as well, but he could already have returned to the stage with Olivia (line 91.1). Sir Toby is silent, 'halting' (line 186). There are now at least eleven people on stage. Does Sir Toby quite realize where he is? Is he drunk again? What kind of hurt is he bearing? Cesario must stand her ground again and not be intimidated by the moment. Orsino speaks to her; perhaps Sir Toby seems too dangerous for Olivia herself to make the first approach. He is dismissive of the Count, and addresses Feste instead. If Feste is already on stage, then his reply may be construed as nonsensical (in response to Sir Toby's drunken confusion); if Feste enters with Sir Toby, then we may see some nurturing taking place, even though the surgeon is too drunk to come (lines 190–3). Sir Toby seems *very* drunk judging from his insult about the surgeon being a 'passey-measures pavan', which may be a drunken slur for 'passe-mezzo pavana' (a slow dance), or (perhaps better) 'passing-measured paynim' (a pagan of notorious degree). This is followed immediately by the heavily ironic 'I hate a drunken rogue.'

196–201.1   Olivia has finally had enough. Sir Andrew steps forward to help his companion with good intentions and even imagines them being bandaged ('dressed') together. Sir Toby seems to growl a public

and brutal betrayal and delivers a tirade of hurtful insults to Sir
Andrew. Are these accompanied by any physical abuse, too? Does Sir
Andrew still manage to help Sir Toby off the stage following Olivia's
instruction? Do her attendants help only Sir Toby, or both of them
separately? It is unnecessary for Feste or Fabian to leave the stage at
this point (as some editions suggest). Sir Andrew may have a
moment of painful realization that no real friendship exists between
himself and Sir Toby, and leave the stage, lagging behind, in the same
or the opposite direction, with fragile independence.

201.1–215   Enter Sebastian. Suddenly the mood and focus change,
and the earlier approaches towards explanation now begin to culminate in looming and inevitable reunion, with the appearance of a
single character. Crucially, we see him *not* notice Cesario straight-
away, and he addresses Olivia, making clear that he was the man who
injured Sir Toby. Sebastian recognizes a change in her countenance
(line 205), and begins to make further excuses for his treatment of Sir
Toby.

   This moment could be staged so that everyone can see
Sebastian, but he *can't* see Cesario. Perhaps Cesario is positioned
with her back to Sebastian. The audience's attention may move
among all the main characters present, but it is Cesario whose reaction may be the most studied. Orsino's reaction (lines 209–10) may
be played out to the audience, as an aside, or may be spoken to one
or more of the on-stage characters. He gives an objective, visual
description of the scenic impression as it appears to the audience,
building a bridge from his character out into the auditorium.
Sebastian sees Antonio (or did we think he was about to see his
sister?). Perhaps this takes him a little closer to Cesario in stage
terms, building towards the dramatic climax. Sebastian speaks
excitedly, musically gasping a succession of open vowels (line 211),
before shaping his comparable suffering into coherent utterance
(lines 212–13). Antonio hears from Sebastian precisely what he
longed to hear from Cesario, and can hardly believe it. He seems
very unsure about this sudden expression of emotional relief and
his reaction, according to Sebastian, could even sound terrified, as
though he's seen a ghost (lines 214–15).

216–19   Antonio expresses his astonishment at seeing the two twins on stage. To hear his words after Orsino's words acts almost as an emotional valve of release for the audience, as Shakespeare prepares us for Sebastian seeing his lost sister. Cesario has not yet spoken herself, but perhaps she has tried to, or perhaps the shock at seeing her brother has stupefied her into silence. We may see her lost for words for the first time thus far. Antonio's comparison of the twins' similarities to a halved apple brings a pastoral mood to the moment. There is, too, something domestic, ordinary, and everyday about the image. At what point does Sebastian see Cesario? This could be during Antonio's reply (lines 216–18). Olivia's interjection could bring the house down, producing more laughter as an emotional release (especially if she speaks the line with gratification, out to the audience), or she may be able to sustain a heightened mood of the miraculous.

220–5   The actor playing Sebastian can pause for as long as he chooses before delivering his next lines to Cesario. Do they move towards each other slowly? It may be helpful to think about the dramatic texture of the next few moments taking place out of time, in a heightened sphere of emotional reality, with the script representing the characters' inner thoughts and feelings rather than only their verbal expression. The language we hear seems to defer any immediate physical contact. Instead we hear the miraculous being articulated (lines 220–5), a present expression of Sebastian's thought processes: 'I don't have a brother, I am not omnipresent, I used to have a sister, but she was cruelly drowned.' Are there tears in his eyes as Sebastian refers to 'blind waves'? If both twins' facial expressions change through their heightened emotion, this could be a way of their seeming more similar to each other in appearance.

226–34   Perhaps Cesario is breathless with emotion before she barely manages to speak (the first time since line 183), and it's an incomplete sentence: 'Of Messaline.' By naming her father and her brother, it is as if she is gradually making emotional and intellectual sense of the moment. The man before her looks like her brother, but she can't quite make herself believe that he is. If ghosts exist, then one

is before her. Perhaps in Cesario's shock we begin to register a change
in the timbre of her voice at this point, and hear it regaining its feminine quality. Sebastian takes up the word 'spirit', interrupting and
sharing her line of verse. His lines still keep his fullest expression of
emotion at arm's length: 'in that dimension grossly clad / Which
from the womb I did participate' is difficult to follow on first hearing
and could sound overly pedantic. The religious implications of
Sebastian's drawing attention to his body and soul may also evoke an
audience's spiritual sensibilities. Sebastian's speech becomes clearer,
but is still couched in the conditional mood: 'were you a woman…I
should'. The language of externalized emotion may be made more
effective by the twins maintaining their physical distance.

235   Finally she is named! Cesario turns into Viola. A new name is
introduced for everyone to hear in this richly populated public space.
It sounds similar to Olivia, even Malvolio, and the astute listener may
recall Orsino's imaginary 'bank of violets' in the play's opening
speech, or even Sir Toby's 'viol-de-gamboys' (I.iii.23–4). The name
calls to mind an ecclesiastical colour; the violet is also a symbol of
humility. By being named, she becomes real and whole again for
Sebastian, a complete person, and her character becomes newly
inscribed for the audience.

236–52   Viola's is an odd comment that comes out of nowhere, but
is the kind of thing that people may recollect and talk about during a
moment of uncontrollable, almost surreal and mixed emotions. If it
generates laughter, then so much the better. It is Viola's objective way
of proving what she has long hoped to be true, as does the information she shares about the death of her father. We hear her speak her
own name for the first time (line 238).

    Physical contact can be difficult for some people and Viola asks
not to be embraced by her brother until she has carefully gone
through all of the circumstances which have brought them to this
moment. Interestingly, this choice also eschews the possibility of us
seeing two similar looking men embrace (though the actors would
have been a man and a boy in Shakespeare's time). It's possible that
Viola glances at Orsino between lines 243 and 247. The utterance 'I

am Viola' (line 247) could be delivered with high emotion, relief, but at the same time sound like a total affirmation of self. Her avoidance of an embrace does not mean that we do not see them touch. A stroke of the cheek, a hand on the shoulder, a light brush of the hair could contribute greatly to the emotional impact of this reunion. If a production does deny us the opportunity of seeing an embrace between brother and sister we may feel emotionally unrequited, but this seems to be what the text requires.

253–71 Sebastian turns their emotional dialogue out to Olivia, making clear her mistake and her absurd situation. If we see Orsino addressing Olivia (lines 258–60), then it may be to claim his superiority. His addressing Viola ironically as 'boy' may cause a ripple of laughter, but it could also sound like Orsino back-pedalling and protesting his normative heterosexuality. Viola is quick to reply, starting her sentence with the conjunction 'and'. The play seems to be ending. Orsino asks for her hand. If this is the first moment that they have made physical contact, then it could be electrifying. We may even see Orsino and Viola move as if to leave the stage. But then Viola recalls the Captain, kept prisoner by Malvolio. The name itself is enough to bring us in to a new movement of thought and action.

272–92 In the Folio, there is no stage direction for Feste and Fabian to re-enter during Olivia's speech. They could easily have remained on stage from the beginning of the scene. Feste's report of Malvolio is based on his and our first-hand knowledge from Act IV, scene iii. He produces the letter we saw at the start of the scene, and we also learn that he should have delivered it 'today morning'. Depending on the time of day at which this scene is set, Feste may appear to be very late in his delivery of the letter. Either way, he could not care less (lines 279–82). Perhaps we hear him managing to sound quite like Malvolio (line 285); perhaps we see him enjoying his impression of madness a little too much. Feste may even try reading it a second time, before Olivia interrupts and orders him to pass the letter to Fabian (lines 291–2).

293–317 Fabian's reading of the letter is crucial, as it can establish the audience's sympathy for Malvolio before he finally appears, as well as show us how the others in the scene react to news of him. The language is direct and plain (as Orsino observes, line 305), in contrast to its immediate context. Malvolio already sounds humbled, and poetic justice begins with the only person on stage who was present during Malvolio's reading of the letter (Fabian) being sent off to free him from prison.

Olivia takes immediate advantage of the moment of hiatus to try to steer us towards a happy ending again. She seems to direct her speech (lines 307–10) to Orsino (who replies), but supposing these lines were addressed to Sebastian or even Viola? If she speaks them to Orsino, it may be made clear that Olivia is regaining a brother as well. The quadrilateral of the two couples' relationships could undergo very careful and complicated handling during this speech, as we see tensions eased and the balance of power and attraction beginning to settle down.

Olivia offers to pay for and host the wedding ceremony. Orsino offers Viola his hand again (line 316), and there may be on-stage approval and encouragement of this public declaration. Perhaps we see the two couples moving more closely together and Olivia may kiss Viola as she calls her sister (line 317). If so, this is a kiss she has been desiring for a long time (ever since Act I, scene v). Is Antonio still held captive? If Orsino authorizes his release, then now may be an appropriate time to do that. If so, Antonio may take up his place close to Sebastian and begin to know Viola and Olivia.

317.1–335   A happy ending is deferred. The mood changes as we see Malvolio return with Fabian. What physical state is he in? Dirty and unkempt? Or does he look merely dishevelled whilst carrying within him much deeper wounds? Are any physical effects of his confinement discernible in the way he walks, stands, or talks? He may overhear Orsino calling him a 'madman'. He speaks directly. There is an opportunity here for a brief stage echo as we glimpse Malvolio holding again the letter which before he was utterly delighted to read. His speech could have a pre-prepared quality about it. It's the first time we've heard him speak in verse, and there is a slick and polished energy in it, almost as if he's rehearsed this scene many times before in the off-stage reality of his prison cell. He doesn't, for example, give Olivia time to respond during the line 'You can say none of this. Well, grant it then,' yet perhaps we see her trying to do so. Similarly lines 325–35 all make up one sentence, as Malvolio offers an inventory of abuse (which is also a description of Malvolio's journey in miniature, as we have seen it since Act III, scene iv). Yet there are still vestiges of pride. He is still able to look down on those 'lighter' (lesser) than himself. Do we see any kind of reaction from Feste when Malvolio recalls being 'visited by the priest'; do we see any reaction from the priest himself (who hasn't yet left the stage)?

336–46   Olivia has been looking at the letter during some or all of Malvolio's speech. It gives her an excuse to avoid the pain of looking him in the eye. Perhaps we notice that Maria is not present on stage during this final scene (unless she has entered as one of Olivia's attendants, line 91.1). Malvolio may begin to react angrily at hearing about her involvement, since Olivia asks him 'Prithee be content,' before promising full justice.

346–60   Fabian suddenly steps forward and speaks in verse, for the first time. This scene finds new voices and creates new identities, which add to the sense that we are approaching the end. We hear a confession until line 354 (though there is no mention of Sir Andrew), and the sudden news that Sir Toby has married Maria (jokingly anticipated at II.v.171). How may Olivia react? Feste may already know, but no one else present on stage knows Sir Toby well enough to be especially interested. For the audience, the news may be a bolt from the blue, or it may seem like an inevitable but still surprising and inappropriate outcome. Olivia's single-line response sounds affectionate, and may lead to appropriate physical contact between her and Malvolio. Her use of 'poor fool' and 'baffled' makes Malvolio at once an object of affection and one whom she compares to a knight (baffling was the formal, public disgracing of a knight). Perhaps she even moves closer to him, and offers him nurture of some kind, and therefore approbation and forgiveness.

361–8   Feste, who has remained silent for just under seventy lines,

steps forward to speak. Perhaps he connects the sound of the word
'baffled' with a report he's heard of Malvolio's reaction to the letter
(II.v.153), which he now quotes from. The fact that he can, also
suggests that the letter itself has acquired some sort of highly memo-
rable status in the off-stage reality. Or, it may simply seem unnerving
and uncanny that Feste should start recollecting Malvolio's stupidity
now. Does Feste speak directly to Malvolio, perhaps as a stage whisper in his ear? Or perhaps his speech is spoken publicly to all present.
His confession about being Sir Topaz, though, seems intended for
Malvolio alone. Overheard it may be, but it's only meaningful to the
two of them.

We hear him imitate Malvolio's voice in prison with words that
Malvolio never actually said on stage. Feste paraphrases Malvolio's
put-down of I.v.78–82 (only meaningful to the two of them and
Olivia). There is violent energy in the word 'gagged', and the actor
playing Feste can choose to be as brutal as he likes in his delivery of
it. The audience is drawn in by Feste's comments, and then suddenly
held at arm's length, as is everyone else on stage, with the line: 'and
thus the whirligig of time brings in his revenges'. The actor playing
Feste can say it as slowly and as carefully as he likes.

Does it sound sinister, fateful, regretful, patronizing? Perhaps it is
whispered as though for Malvolio alone. It is a final moment of
humiliation. Is Malvolio hanging his head in shame, or is it raised and
defiant? Perhaps he pauses and starts to leave before his next line. Or
he may remain quite still and poised. Malvolio can choose his
moment carefully and he can sound as chilling or as broken as the
moment warrants: 'I'll be revenged on the whole pack of you.' 'Pack'
is suggestive of wolves or dogs, and its plosive can be spat out with
the venom of anger, revenge, and self-loathing. The line may be delivered to Feste, but suggests, rather, a derisive inclusion of everyone
present. In fact, there are only Fabian and Feste (and possibly Olivia)
present on stage for whom Malvolio's revenge is appropriate. The
line is a gift to the actor and brings the role to a powerful climax in a
single moment.

368.1–78   Although no exit is marked for Malvolio in the Folio,
Orsino's 'pursue him' suggests that Malvolio leaves and that some-

one, possibly Fabian, obeys. Some productions may decide to keep Malvolio on stage (cutting Orsino's line, or making it sound like a threat of interrogation still to come), quietly suffering, and show him being absorbed back into the status quo of Olivia's court. She goes on to speak about him in the third person, which implies either Malvolio's absence, or perhaps some physical nurturing on her part.

The captain is mentioned for the third time during this scene (see also lines 248 and 268). For Orsino, he is crucial. He has Viola's woman's clothes and can give a further account of the shipwreck. He is, however, as we've already learned, a prisoner of Malvolio's, so perhaps his revenge may involve Malvolio not giving up the captain quite so easily.

Orsino looks towards a happier, 'golden time' of marriage celebrations for the two couples. He wants them all to remain in Olivia's home, and addresses her as 'sweet sister'. We hear Cesario named again (it will take practice before Orsino gets into the habit of saying Viola), a critical distance between the Duke and someone who looks like a man. Orsino's final couplet looks ahead to Viola dressing differently, so that he can behave differently towards her, and see his 'fancy' for another man become safely reformed into 'fancy' for a woman.

378.1–end   Feste remains on stage while everyone else leaves. How? Do they leave during his song, perhaps after he's sung a verse to individuals, or groups? Or do we see them clear the stage, leaving him alone to sing to the audience? How, if at all, is Antonio released from the First Officer? Does he join the two couples? Is he excluded or admitted into their closed circle of happiness? Do the couples dance during the song? How are these final moments exuberant? Or, do they strike a subtly shaded sense of compromise and inspire mixed emotions?

Feste's song is nostalgic but unsentimental. He recalls a lost childhood and his coming to manhood, his taking a wife, his decline into drinking, and all this is set against the persistent reminder of the present rain and cold of human existence. The song acts as a moment of reflection on the play we've just seen. We may recall Viola taking upon herself 'man's estate', the drunkenness of Sir Toby, his marrying

Maria, the other two couples who are about to marry; and the constant reiteration of the wind and the rain (perhaps recalling the endurance of Olivia's own natural beauty I.v.227) makes this song tempest-tossed, like the shipwreck itself.

The final verse takes us back in time to the start of creation, throwing the responsibility onto each member of the audience and his or her place in the great scheme of things. Feste reminds us that we have merely been watching actors striving to please us, as we must strive to please each other, whatever life brings.

The song ends and our satisfaction may seem complicated, melancholic, as though there is a piece missing. Perhaps we recollect that the play also began with music and the search for romance, that the wheel has now come full circle, and that we, like all those on stage, have in some way been changed; our hearts might have broken, and now be differently restored.

Bibliography

References and Further Reading

This section aims to recommend reading that will extend and deepen understanding of the areas covered in this book. It includes short descriptions of works which may be particularly useful and lists other works cited.

Barton, Anne, '*As You Like It* and *Twelfth Night*: Shakespeare's Sense of an Ending', in Anne Barton, *Essays, Mainly Shakespearian* (Cambridge: Cambridge University Press, 1994): a fine appreciation of Shakespeare's comic climax.

Barton, John, *Playing Shakespeare* (London: Methuen, 1984): an account of nine workshops with famous actors, and a companion to the Channel 4 television series. The chapter on *Twelfth Night* is based on episode six.

Bate, Jonathan (ed.), *The Romantics on Shakespeare* (Harmondsworth: Penguin, 1992): a useful anthology of influential criticism by great writers.

Bell, John, *Bell's Edition of Shakespeare's Plays: As they are now presented in the Theatres Royal in London*, vol. 5 (London: John Bell, 1774).

Berry, Ralph, *Changing Styles in Shakespeare* (London: George Allen & Unwin, 1981). The chapter on *Twelfth Night* shows how the laughter in productions has changed since 1894.

Billington, Michael (ed.), with Bill Alexander, John Barton, John Caird, and Terry Hands, *Directors' Shakespeare: Approaches to 'Twelfth Night'* (London: Nick Hern, 1990): a highly engaging and wide-ranging five-way conversation about many different aspects of the play.

Bloom, Harold (ed.), *William Shakespeare's 'Twelfth Night'*, Modern Critical Interpretations (New York: Chelsea House Publications, 1987): includes many helpful and representative pieces from 1961–85, some of which are referred to in Chapter 5.

Bradley, David, *From Text to Performance in the Elizabethan Theatre: Preparing the Play for the Stage* (Cambridge: Cambridge University Press, 1992): a discussion of playwrights, companies and theatre practice, with statistical cast lists of public theatre plays from 1475 to 1625.

Brockbank, Philip (ed.), *Players of Shakespeare 1* (Cambridge: Cambridge University Press, 1985; repr. 1996): includes an insightful autobiographical account of Donald Sinden's 1969 performance of Malvolio.

Brontë, Emily, *Wuthering Heights* (London: Penguin, 1965; repr. 1985).

Brown, John Russell, *Shakespeare's Plays in Performance* (London: Edward Arnold, 1966): an innovatory study with a chapter on *Twelfth Night*.

——, 'Representing Sexuality in Shakespeare's Plays', in Catherine M. S. Alexander and Stanley Wells (eds), *Shakespeare and Sexuality* (Cambridge: Cambridge University Press, 2001), pp. 168–82. First published in *New Theatre Quarterly*, 13 (1997), Brown's essay gives a practical overview of some possible theatrical effects relating to sexuality across a range of plays. It is reprinted in a collection of thematically related articles mainly from *Shakespeare Survey* from 1992 to 1996.

——, *Shakespeare and the Theatrical Event* (Basingstoke: Palgrave Macmillan, 2002): a dynamic survey and guide to how to approach Shakespeare as an imagined performance, which discusses the possibilities and contingencies of live theatre.

Bullough, Geoffrey (ed.), *Narrative and Dramatic Sources of Shakespeare*, 8 vols (London: Routledge & Kegan Paul, 1957–75): the standard reference work for source material. *Twelfth Night* is covered in vol. 2, which includes 'Apolonius and Silla' and extracts of *The Famous History of Parismus* (both in old spelling), and a shortened translation of *Gl'Ingannati*.

Clayton, Tom, Susan Brock and Vicente Forés (eds), *Shakespeare and the Mediterranean* (Newark: University of Delaware Press, 2001): a truly international collection of essays, including a retrospective on John Gielgud's career by Michael Coveney, an article on Trevor Nunn's film of *Twelfth Night* by Ann Jennalie Cook, and an article on Renaissance ideas about Illyria by Goran Stanivukovic.

Cottrell, John, *Laurence Oliver* (London: Weidenfeld & Nicolson, 1975).

Craig, Edward Gordon, *Henry Irving* (London: J. M. Dent, 1930): a critical biography of Irving's career and stagecraft by someone who adored him.

Draper, John W., *The Twelfth Night of Shakespeare's Audience* (Stanford, CA: Stanford University Press, 1950): a detailed character analysis relating to the historical context, setting, costume, and mood.

Everett, Barbara, 'Two Damned Cruces: *Othello* and *Twelfth Night*', in *Young Hamlet: Essays on Shakespeare's Tragedies* (Oxford: Clarendon Press, 1989). This essay, first published in *Review of English Studies* (May 1986), suggests 'lemon-coloured' as a textual emendation for the colour of Sir Andrew Aguecheek's stockings.

Fielding, Emma, *Twelfth Night*, Actors on Shakespeare (London: Faber and Faber, 2002): a useful account of Viola, and Fielding's theatrical process in playing the role.

Gielgud, John, *An Actor in His Time* (London: Sidgwick & Jackson, 1979).

——, *Gielgud's Letters*, ed. Richard Mangan (London: Weidenfeld and Nicolson, 2004): an invaluable collection of insights into Gielgud's life, work, and twentieth-century theatrical history.

Granville-Barker, Harley, *Prefaces to Shakespeare*, vol. 6 (London: B. T. Batsford, 1974). He is always worth reading on Shakespeare in performance and his advice can always be practically realized.

Hall, Peter, 'Introduction', *Twelfth Night*, ed. M. R. Ridley, with a glossary by Jean Rook, Folio Society, based on the New Temple Shakespeare (London: Folio Society, 1966).

Hammond, Paul, *Figuring Sex Between Men from Shakespeare to Rochester* (Oxford: Clarendon Press, 2002): an excellent discussion of seventeenth-century literary presentations of sex between men, with a section on *Twelfth Night*.

Heywood, Thomas, *An Apology for Actors* (London: Shakespeare

Society, 1841): a vindication of the stage and of the professional theatre, first published in 1612.

Hiatt, Charles, *Ellen Terry* (London: George Bell, 1899): a useful account of Terry's major roles, including a chapter on Viola.

Hodges, C. Walter, *Enter the Whole Army: A Pictorial Study of Shakespearean Staging, 1576–1616* (Cambridge: Cambridge University Press, 1999). Hodges combines his own unique and fascinating insights with charm as he suggests practical solutions to the early staging of Shakespeare's plays.

Hotson, Leslie, *The First Night of 'Twelfth Night'* (London: Rupert Hart-Davis, 1954): an engaging, thoroughly well-researched, but unlikely historical sweep in quest to identify the original occasion for which Shakespeare wrote the play.

Hughes, Alan, *Henry Irving, Shakespearean* (Cambridge: Cambridge University Press, 1981): an invaluable study of Irving's Shakespearian career.

Irving, Henry (ed.), *Twelfth Night; or What You Will: A comedy in five acts, by William Shakespeare, as arranged for the stage by Henry Irving and presented at the Lyceum Theatre, 8 July 1884* (London: Chiswick Press, 1884).

Jackson, Russell, and Robert Smallwood (eds), *Players of Shakespeare 2* (Cambridge: Cambridge University Press, 1988): includes an insightful autobiographical account of Zoë Wanamaker's 1983 performance of Viola.

Jones, Emrys, *The New Oxford Book of Sixteenth-Century Verse* (Oxford: Oxford University Press, 1991): an anthology of poetry which is useful for understanding the lyrical context of the play.

Kerrigan, John, 'Secrecy and Gossip in *Twelfth Night*', in John Kerrigan, *On Shakespeare and Modern Literature* (Oxford: Oxford University Press, 2001), pp. 89–112. First published in *Shakespeare Survey 50* (1997), this is a subtle and worthwhile literary–historical exploration.

King, T. J., *Casting Shakespeare's Plays: London Actors and Their Roles, 1590–1642* (Cambridge: Cambridge University Press, 1992): a useful presentation and discussion of casting charts for all of Shakespeare's plays.

Latham, Robert and William Mathews (eds), *The Diary of Samuel Pepys,*

11 vols (London: George Bell and Sons, vols 1–8; Bell and Hyman, vols 9–11, 1970–83): vols 2, 4 and 9 are cited.

Maguolias, Michael (ed.), *Shakespearean Criticism*, vol. 26 (New York: Gale Research, 1995).

Manningham, John, *The Diary of John Manningham of the Middle Temple, 1602–3*, ed. Robert Parker Sorlien (Hanover, NH: University of New England Press, 1976): an invaluable edition of Manningham's eye-witness accounts and anecdotes of Shakespeare, his contemporaries, and the world they lived in.

Masefield, John, *William Shakespeare* (London: Williams & Norgate, 1911; rev. 1912; repr. 1921).

Montaigne, Michel de, *Essays*, trans. John Florio, ed. A. R. Waller, 3 vols (London: J. M. Dent, 1910; repr. 1935): a translation from Shakespeare's own period, of Montaigne's intellectual, philosophical and psychological enquiries.

Muir, Kenneth, *Shakespeare's Sources: Comedies and Tragedies* (London: Methuen, 1957): an overview of Shakespeare's raw material with a chapter on *Twelfth Night*.

Nunn, Trevor, *William Shakespeare's Twelfth Night: A Screenplay* (London: Methuen Drama, 1996). Apart from the film script, there is an introductory essay by Nunn about the project.

O'Connor, Garry (ed.), *Olivier in Celebration* (London: Hodder & Stoughton, 1987).

Orgel, Stephen, *Impersonations: The Performance of Gender in Shakespeare's England* (Cambridge: Cambridge University Press, 1996): a discussion which seeks to make visible how gender and sexuality were staged and accepted.

Palmer, D. J. (ed.), *Shakespeare: Twelfth Night*, Casebook series (Basingstoke: Macmillan, 1972): includes many helpful and representative pieces from 1602 to 1969, some of which are referred to in Chapter 5.

Paster, Gail Kern, *Humoring the Body: Emotions and the Shakespearean Stage* (Chicago: University of Chicago Press, 2004): a way of reading the Renaissance self and body through an understanding of physiology, with a section on *Twelfth Night*.

Pemberton, T. Edgar, *Ellen Terry and Her Sisters* (London: C. Arthur Pearson, 1902).

Pennington, Michael, *Twelfth Night: A User's Guide* (London: Nick Hern, 2000): a director's scene-by-scene interpretation of the play in performance.

Pollard, A. W. and G. R. Redgrave, *A Short Title Catalogue of Books Printed in England, Scotland, and Ireland and of English Books Printed Abroad, 1475–1640*, 2nd edn, ed. W. A. Jackson, F. S. Ferguson and Katherine F. Pantzer, 3 vols (London: Bibliographical Society, 1986–91): a cornerstone of Renaissance scholarship which systematically lists all the printed books of the period and can be cross-referenced against the Ann Arbor microfilm collection for consultation of the works, photographed from rare books.

Potter, Lois, *Twelfth Night: Text and Performance* (Basingstoke: Macmillan, 1985): a useful guide to exploring the play's theatre history, which includes a study of four productions through the 1970s and early 1980s.

Shaw, Bernard, *Shaw on Shakespeare*, ed. Edwin Wilson (London: E. P. Dutton, 1961; repr. Applause, 1989): an anthology of the theatre review and other pieces by Bernard Shaw, which covers a wide range of plays.

Smallwood, Robert (ed.), *Players of Shakespeare 5* (Cambridge: Cambridge University Press, 2003): includes an insightful autobiographical account of Zoë Waites's and Matilda Ziegler's 2003 performances of Viola and Olivia.

Smith, Bruce (ed.), *Twelfth Night or What You Will: Texts and Contexts* (Boston and New York: Bedford/St Martin's, 2001): an edition of the play edited by David Bevington and an anthology of extracts from a variety of sources to help view the play in its original historical and anthropological contexts.

Speaight, Robert, 'Shakespeare in Britain, 1974', *Shakespeare Quarterly*, 25 (1974), pp. 389–94.

Stubbes, Philip, *The Anatomie of Abuses*, ed. Margaret Jane Kidnie (Tempe, Arizona: Center for Medieval and Renaissance Studies, in conjunction with the Renaissance English Text Society, 2002): a lively edition of the classic puritan polemic.

Suzman, Janet, *Acting with Shakespeare: The Comedies*, Applause Acting Series (New York: Applause, 1996): a practical guide to performance, with a section on *Twelfth Night*.

Taylor, Gary, *Reinventing Shakespeare* (London: Hogarth Press, 1990; repr. Vintage, 1991): a cultural history of Shakespeare criticism from the Restoration to the late twentieth century.

Terry, Ellen, *The Story of My Life* (London: Hutchinson [1908]): a classic autobiography and overview of a great life and career.

Terry, Ellen, and Bernard Shaw, *Ellen Terry and Bernard Shaw: A Correspondence*, ed. Christopher St John (London: Max Reinhardt, 1949; repr. 1952). Although not explicitly relating to *Twelfth Night*, these are some of the best of all theatrical letters and deepen our knowledge of Irving, Terry, and Shaw, and a whole period of British theatre.

Thomson, Peter, 'The Smallest Season: the Royal Shakespeare Company at Stratford, 1974', in *Shakespeare Survey 28*, ed. Kenneth Muir (Cambridge: Cambridge University Press, 1975), pp. 137–48.

Wells, Stanley, *Royal Shakespeare* (Manchester: Manchester University Press, 1976): four major studies of four major Royal Shakespeare Company productions, including John Barton's *Twelfth Night*, 1969.

—— , *Twelfth Night: Critical Essays* (New York: Garland Publishing, 1986): includes many helpful and representative pieces from 1916 to 1976, some of which are referred to in Chapter 5.

—— (ed.), *Shakespeare in the Theatre: An Anthology of Criticism* (Oxford: Clarendon Press, 1997): a richly supplied anthology of responses by writers, critics and reviewers to Shakespeare in the theatre from 1700 to 1996.

—— , *Shakespeare: For All Time* (Basingstoke: Palgrave Macmillan, 2002): an overview of four centuries of thought, criticism, and creative responses to Shakespeare.

—— , *Looking for Sex in Shakespeare* (Cambridge: Cambridge University Press, 2004): how to do it, and how not to do it, including a discussion of the Antonio/Sebastian relationship.

—— and Lena Orlin (eds), *Shakespeare: An Oxford Guide* (Oxford: Oxford University Press, 2003): contains a helpful essay by William C. Carroll about the theories of romantic comedy, with a reading of *Twelfth Night*.

White, R. S. (ed.), *New Casebooks: Twelfth Night* (Basingstoke: Macmillan, 1996): includes many helpful and representative pieces from 1979–93, some of which are referred to in Chapter 5.

Woolf, Virginia, *The Moment and Other Essays* (London: Hogarth Press, 1947): contains an essay on Ellen Terry.

Woudhuysen, H. R. (ed.), *The Penguin Book of Renaissance Verse, 1509–1659*, selected with an introduction by David Norbrook (London: Allen Lane, Penguin Press, 1992): an anthology of poetry which is useful for understanding the lyrical context of the play.

Editions

Brown, John Russell (ed.), *Twelfth Night*, Applause Shakespeare (New York: Applause, 2001): a clearly printed text on the left-hand side, with a useful performance commentary on the right.

Dunno, Elizabeth Story (ed.), *Twelfth Night*, Cambridge Shakespeare, 3 (Cambridge: Cambridge University Press, 1985): a usefully illustrated and helpful introduction.

Furness, Horace Howard (ed.), *Twelfe Night, or, What You Will*, New Variorum, 4th edn (Philadelphia: J. B. Lippincott, 1901): an invaluable edition which collates and offers a digest of previous texts and criticism.

Lothian, J. M. and T. W. Craik (eds), *Twelfth Night*, Arden 2nd series (London: Methuen, 1975; repr. Routledge, 1995): a full edition, strong on textual matters, with a useful introduction.

Mahood, M. M. (ed.), *Twelfth Night*, New Penguin Shakespeare (Harmondsworth: Penguin, 1968; repr. with additions, 1995): a clearly printed text (good for memorizing), with a helpful introduction and notes. A revised edition with a new introduction by Michael Dobson, further reading section, and a section on the play in performance, was published in 2005.

Warren, Roger, and Stanley Wells (eds), *Twelfth Night*, Oxford Shakespeare (Oxford: Oxford University Press, 1994): a wonderful commentary and radical text, with a new edition of the songs printed as an appendix, by the composer and musician James Walker. This edition is used as the textual reference throughout this book when citing the play.

Wells, Stanley, and Gary Taylor, with John Jowett and William Montgomery (eds), *The Oxford Shakespeare: The Complete Works*, 2nd edn (Oxford: Clarendon Press, 2005). The first edition appeared in 1986. The Oxford Shakespeare is still the most radical and interesting text of Shakespeare's complete works available, which took scholarly editing into another realm with firm but brave principles. It has yet to be bettered.

Wilson, John Dover (ed.), *Twelfth Night*, New Cambridge Shakespeare, 2 (Cambridge: Cambridge University Press, 1930): a beautifully printed text with a helpful introduction and notes.

Films and audio recordings

Although some of the older productions are no longer commercially available, they can be consulted in libraries, or purchased second-hand on the internet.

Twelfth Night, dir. by John Gorrie, BBC, 1979 (Alec McCowen as Malvolio and Felicity Kendal as Viola). This well spoken and safe production is set (as was Peter Hall's 1958 Stratford production) in the Caroline period of Cavaliers and Roundheads.

The following films are discussed in Chapter 4:

Twelfth Night, dir. for television by Paul Kafno (from a stage production dir. by Kenneth Branagh), Thames Television, 1988.
Twelfth Night, dir. by Trevor Nunn, Circus and BBC films, 1996.
Twelfth Night, dir. by Tim Supple, Projector Production, 2003

Audio recordings are an efficient way of getting to know a play well, and a variety of them can help the language to sound freshly minted. Below are just a few recommendations.

Twelfth Night, dir. by George Rylands, Argo, 1961 (Tony Church as Malvolio; Dorothy Tutin as Viola and Patrick Wymark as Sir Toby, both also played these roles in Peter Hall's 1958 Stratford production).
Twelfth Night, dir. Howard Sackler, Caedmon, 1961 (Paul Scofield as Malvolio; Siobhan McKenna as Viola).

Twelfth Night, dir. by Clive Brill, Arkangel, 1998 (Julian Glover as Malvolio; Niamh Cusack as Viola).

Twelfth Night, dir. by Richard Eyre, BBC Radio Collection, 1999 (Hugh Ross as Malvolio; Anne-Marie Duff as Viola).

Twelfth Night, dir. by David Timson, Naxos Audio Books, 1999 (Christopher Godwin as Malvolio; Stella Gonet as Viola).

Index

desire (sexual), 8, 12–14, 16, 18,
     19–20, 22, 24, 25, 44–5, 46–8,
     51–3, 54, 55–8, 61–5, 67–8,
     76–84, 86, 87, 88, 91, 94–5, 96,
     98–9, 100, 104, 107–9, 118,
     119–24, 130–1, 134, 136, 137, 149,
     152, 155–6, 161, 162, 166
Digges, Leonard, 7, 67
Dodd, Mr, 72
Dowland, John, 28
Draper, John W., 70
Dudley, William, 46

Ejiotor, Chiwetel, 63
Elizabeth I, Queen, 4
English Shakespeare Company,
     77–8
Evans, Bertrand, 80
Everett, Barbara, 6, 84
Eyre, Sir Richard, 75

Faulkner, Trader, 44
Fenton, George, 51
Fielding, Emma, 76–7
Fisher, Mr D., 37
Fleay, F. G., 6
Folio (1623), 6–7, 67, 133, 161, 164
Forde, Emanuel, 10, 22–5
Fraser, Meg, 56
Freud, Sigmund, 69
Friedrich, Caspar David, 34
Furness, Horace Howard, 68

gender, 2, 7, 12, 15, 17, 21, 23, 25, 32,
     35, 37, 41, 44, 47, 48, 50, 51–5,
     62, 65, 68, 72, 73, 76, 85, 88,
     89–90, 91, 94, 96, 97, 98, 102,
     105, 109, 110–11, 118, 119–22,
     127–8, 132, 144, 146, 148, 154,
     160, 165

Gentleman, Francis, 70
Gervinus, G. G., 68
Gibbs, Anne, 7
Gielgud, Sir John, 38–45, 58, 60
Gill, Peter, 45–53
Gl'Ingannati, 2, 10, 16–22, 83
Gl'Inganni, 2
Globe Theatre, 2, 3, 29, 135
Goethe, Johann Wolfgang von, 79
Grant, Richard E., 62
Granville-Barker, Harley, 40, 72–3,
     74
Gray's Inn, 1
Greenblatt, Stephen, 82–3
Greene, Graham, 42

Hall, Brian, 49
Hall, Sir Peter, 73, 75
Hammond, Paul, 83–4
Hampton Court, 29
Hands, Terry, 77
Hawthorne, Sir Nigel, 62
Hayes, Patricia, 48, 51
Hazlitt, William, 67
Henson, Nicky, 56
Heywood, Thomas, 28
Hilliard, Nicholas, 48
Hodges, C. Walter, 3
Hotson, Leslie, 4, 28
Howard, Jean E., 76
Howe, Mr H., 34
Hughes, Alan, 33–4
Hunt, Leigh, 78

Irving, Sir Henry, 30–8, 58

James I, King, 7
Jameson, Anna, 68
Jenkins, Harold, 80
Jhutti, Ronny, 63